D1111093

Seminary Formation

Seminary Formation

Recent History—
Current Circumstances—
New Directions

Katarina Schuth, OSF

Foreword by
Archbishop Blase J. Cupich

Commentaries by
Ronald Rolheiser, OMI
Thomas Walters
Leon M. Hutton
Barbara E. Reid, OP
Msgr. Peter Vaccari

LITURGICAL PRESS
Collegeville, Minnesota

www.litpress.org

Cover design by Monica Bokinskie. Photo: Mount St. Mary's Seminary of the West | Cincinnati, Ohio | Preparing Men for the Priesthood since 1829. MTSM Seminarians (left to right): Eric Roush, Sean Wilson, Alex McCullough, and Timothy Fahey. Used with permission.

1   2   3   4   5   6   7   8   9

Library of Congress Cataloging-in-Publication Data

Names: Schuth, Katarina, author.
Title: Seminary formation : recent history-current circumstances-new directions / Katarina Schuth, O.S.F. ; commentaries by Ron Rolheiser, O.M.I, Thomas Walters, Rev. Leon Hutton, Barbara Reid, O.P., Rev. Msgr. Peter Vaccari.
Description: Collegeville, Minnesota : Liturgical Press, 2016. | Includes bibliographical references and index.
Identifiers: LCCN 2016009627 (print) | LCCN 2016031287 (ebook) | ISBN 9780814648001 | ISBN 9780814648278 (ebook)
Subjects: LCSH: Catholic theological seminaries—United States. | Theology—Study and teaching—Catholic Church. | Theology—Study and teaching—United States.
Classification: LCC BX905 .S425 2016 (print) | LCC BX905 (ebook) | DDC 230.07/3273—dc23
LC record available at https://lccn.loc.gov/2016009627

With deep gratitude to Pope Francis
for his great inspiration to the church and the world
and for his compassionate care for the people of God

Contents

List of Tables

Foreword

The year 1989 was a year of a happy coincidence. I was appointed rector/president of the Pontifical College Seminary and Sr. Katarina Schuth published her pioneering study of Roman Catholic seminaries and theologates, *Reason for the Hope*. It was a book that challenged me and my colleagues at other seminaries to reevaluate our programs on a number of levels. For instance, we better understood from the feedback on her research the important contribution women were making on our academic and formational faculties. Likewise, she highlighted the benefits of evaluating readiness for orders based more on discerning gifts rather than impediments.

For the nearly thirty years since that book, Katarina has earned a well-deserved reputation as the person who knows more about Catholic seminaries and schools of theology in this country than anyone on the planet. Her research method is thorough and meticulous, something I came to know firsthand as she worked on her second book, *Seminaries, Theologates, and the Future of Church Ministry*, published a decade later. In those years, she and her team visited nearly every school of theology at that time, close to forty in all. Rectors, presidents, faculty, and vocation directors were asked to respond to questionnaires. She also conducted personal interviews of students, faculty, administrators, and staff. To be sure, her approach created new demands for those participating in her research, but they were demands that gave her work credibility. We recognized that this is a person who was not going to waste our time.

Over the years, Katarina has demonstrated an admirable ability to gather and organize data with the kind of detailed precision that borders on the scrupulous. Her presentation of facts is sophisticatedly synthetic, crisply composed, informative, and insightful. With all of this she brings a deep love for the church, for priesthood and scholarship.

With *Seminary Formation: Recent History—Current Circumstances—New Directions* Katarina builds on her solid reputation as a scholarly researcher. Her goal is to update her earlier research, specifically by appraising how seminaries and schools of theology have changed from 1985 to the present.

Part I situates the present state of seminaries and theologates in the era of the Second Vatican Council. She identifies a shift with each successive edition of the *Program of Priestly Formation (PPF)*. With the passage of time, those involved in this document's subsequent revision were less personally connected to the council. Consequently, as distance from the council increases, its documents receive less attention and more focus is given to the writings of St. Pope John Paul II.

Katarina presents the bulk of her research in the next two parts. No stone is left unturned. She examines almost every aspect of theologate-level schools, including their structures and missions, by providing information about boards and their membership, faculty and administrators (part II). Despite her remarks about the waning impact of the council on *PPF* revisions, she maintains a commendable objectivity to notice the ongoing influence of Vatican II on theologates. For instance, she remarks that diocesan seminaries have enlarged their missions to include enrollment of religious order seminarians and lay students. They focus on parish ministry and the need to train priests to pastor communities.

In part III, her review of the organizational aspects of theologates is complemented by a careful assessment of student enrollments and backgrounds of both seminarians and lay students. Attention especially is given to the evolution and development of degree programs, as well as what is involved in human, spiritual, intellectual, and pastoral formation, and how they have changed.

The data Katarina presents on the decline of enrollment since the peak years of the 1960s is sobering. In 1969, there were 4,876 diocesan seminarians and 3,283 religious order candidates, for a total of 8,159 men studying for the priesthood. Over the next 15 years, the total number dropped to 3,813 and continued to decline, albeit less dramatically. Most recent enrollment, in 2014, was 3,650, divided between diocesan candidates at 2,799 and religious candidates at 851.

Readers will find her work very engaging and even conversational. Throughout her presentation she organizes the data into a narrative, explaining the evolution of the changes and the possible reasons why they occurred. This allows her to offer insights about new directions for the future in part IV.

As I think back on that year of happy coincidence, and the nearly three decades since then, I find that Katarina's work is impressive on a number of levels. First, she has maintained a discipline in her method of research over the years, which makes it easy for her to make connections with the data she gathered in each succeeding project. Secondly, by giving us a common frame of reference and a language to engage each other, Katarina has facilitated conversations among those involved in seminary work. We literally were able to see how each other was doing, and that we had a lot to gain by sharing information with each other. As the title of her first book suggests, she also gave me and other rectors reasons for hope, as we discovered in her work that the concerns and challenges we faced were indeed common and could be best addressed in a collaborative way. It is not too much to suggest that in these past three decades any significant conversation about seminaries and theologates has been shaped by her research. That includes the work done in preparing the various revisions of *PPF*.

Her research also facilitated conversation with those involved in ministerial formation in other denominations. This resulted in sharing best practices. One particular example is in the area of board development. With her advice and assistance, many Catholic seminaries benefited from generous grants from the Lilly Endowment that funded board development retreats. Much of this was due to Katarina's solid reputation with Lilly and her credibility in the Catholic seminary world.

Sr. Katarina has proven to be an able scholar and researcher, but as I think about how she writes, there is another word that comes to mind. The Swiss painter of the last century, Paul Klee, once observed that "art doesn't give us things to see; art makes us see." Katarina is a researcher and a scholar, but also an artist. She makes us see. The rest is up to us.

Archbishop Blase J. Cupich
Archdiocese of Chicago

Acknowledgments

After many years of engagement with colleagues in seminary and theologate communities, those who deserve great thanks for assisting me with research and writing are numerous. Beyond the immediate scope of these institutions are many other religious leaders, community members, friends, and family who have been supportive in a variety of ways. The project required cooperation on many levels, but given the limits of space, I will be able to name only some of those who deserve recognition.

As I began research for the book, I was fortunate to have a committee of advisers who have been leaders in seminary education for many years. Their insights and suggestions have added so much to the final product, and beyond that, each of them wrote a commentary for the book: Rev. Ron Rolheiser, OMI, president, Oblate School of Theology; Dr. Thomas Walters, dean emeritus, Saint Meinrad Seminary; Rev. Leon Hutton, dean of Human Formation, St. John's Seminary, Camarillo, California (now pastor); Sr. Barbara Reid, OP, vice president and academic dean, Catholic Theological Union; Rev. Msgr. Peter Vaccari, rector, St. Joseph's Seminary, Dunwoodie, New York. Also on the advisory committee was Msgr. Jeremiah McCarthy, moderator of the Curia for the Diocese of Tucson, who wrote observations on the state of moral theology and on the role of the Association of Theological Schools with Catholic theologates. The broad and dependable advice they offered and their written contributions were priceless. I thank each of them for their time, interest, wise counsel, and friendship.

Adding valuable insights were the leaders of theologates—rectors, presidents, and deans—who responded to a lengthy survey about many aspects of their institutions. Although too numerous to mention by name, I greatly appreciate their candid views and perceptions and their generosity in taking the time to respond fully and willingly to the survey, as well as assisting me in so many other ways through the years. I hope this work accurately reflects their understandings.

I am grateful to the Lilly Endowment, Inc., for again funding my research on Catholic theologates. Their generosity through the years has made it possible for me to have the time and resources to write three other books. On this project, John Wimmer, program director in the Religion Division, has offered encouragement and support for the duration of the grant. Also, I am indebted to Liturgical Press for again publishing my book, especially to Barry Hudock, who has been supportive and patient in guiding me to the conclusion of this project. Dr. Victor Klimoski, former academic dean of the Saint Paul Seminary, edited and commented on the text, improving immensely its intelligibility and clarity. His firsthand knowledge of seminaries adds considerably to the substance of the book. Without the proficient efforts of Catherine Slight, my assistant, this book would be far from complete. She was indefatigable in tracking down every piece of information and persistent in attending to endless details—always with a positive spirit.

Several individuals and organizations make my work more complete and more accurate. Mary L. Gautier, senior research associate at CARA, has been a constant source of knowledge about and understanding of data on seminaries. Her immediate answers to my most obscure questions demonstrate her extraordinary grasp of the subject and her magnanimous friendship in spending time to answer. For more than fifty years CARA has provided quality research on seminaries and many other aspects of the Catholic Church. Dr. Daniel Aleshire, executive director of the Association of Theological Schools, is a valued colleague and friend who has taken unparalleled interest in my research. For twenty-five years he has provided endless opportunities for me to learn about theological education beyond Catholic institutions and to present my research findings in many contexts. I am so grateful to him both personally and professionally.

Religious and academic leaders have contributed in many additional ways. Archbishop Blase Cupich of Chicago, who wrote the foreword for this book, has been a steadfast supporter and thoughtful advocate of my work for many years. He has shown intense interest in seminary formation and has served the church in this endeavor with exceptional competence. Bishop Gerald Kicanas of Tucson, since his days as rector of Mundelein Seminary, has encouraged and supported me on numerous occasions. Msgr. W. Shawn McKnight, as head of the USCCB Committee on Clergy, Consecrated Life, and Vocations, initiated and cooperated with many projects of mutual interest and always included me in his deliberations. The Sulpicians as a group, particularly Rev. Melvin Blanchette, SS, have provided leadership in ongoing education for seminary personnel for over twenty-five years. They have sponsored workshops to educate new seminary formators, that have enhanced my understanding and offered me an opportunity to make presentations at these gatherings.

Other longtime associates and friends remain as unwavering allies: Former Weston Jesuit School of Theology colleagues; Rev. John O'Malley, SJ, Georgetown University; Sr. Mary Sweeney, SC, Rev. Richard Clifford, SJ, and Rev. Randall Sachs, SJ, Boston College; Rev. Edward Vacek, SJ, Loyola University, New Orleans; Rev. Frederic Maples, SJ, Boston; Rev. Donald Senior, CP, president emeritus, Catholic Theological Union; Dr. Deborah Organ, St. Catherine University; and Rev. Kevin O'Neil, CSsR, San Alfonso Retreat House, New Jersey. Colleagues at my own school also have been understanding and thoughtful, making it possible for me to work in an atmosphere conducive to research and writing: Msgr. Aloysius Callaghan, rector and vice president at the Saint Paul Seminary School of Divinity; Dr. Julie Sullivan, president of the University of St. Thomas; and coworkers at the seminary, especially Sr. Paul Therese Saiko, SSND, and at the university, faculty of the departments of Sociology and Theology.

On a personal level, I am so thankful to my friends and family who have endured several years of inattention as I focused on this book. The Sisters of St. Francis, Rochester, Minnesota, my religious community of more than fifty years, have always stood by me. The leaders of the congregation, especially our current leader, Sr. Marilyn Geiger, encouraged and assisted me in every way possible. My small community of Franciscan sisters, Ellen Whelan, Gavin Hagan, Marlene Pinzka, Jean Keniry, Colleen Byron, and Joanne Loecher, have shown incredible patience in listening to my many tales of seminary life. All of them, along with our sisters Yvette Kaiser, June Kaiser, and Margaret Boler, are valued friends.

My family grows larger every year and all of them have demonstrated enthusiasm, thoughtfulness, and patience as I work too long and miss too many happy family occasions. I attribute the joy that pervades my life to all of them—especially my living brothers, Robert, Michael, and Matthew, and those deceased, John, Edward, and Paul, along with my parents. Each day for the three years of this project I have prayed for them and asked God for protection and strength for all of us: "Let us not grow tired of doing good, for in due time we shall reap our harvest, if we do not give up. So then, while we have the opportunity, let us do good to all, but especially to those who belong to the family of the faith" (Gal 6:9-10). My profound thanks to all who in any way have been there for me. God has blessed me abundantly with faith, family, and friends.

Frequently Used Documents, Abbreviations, and Terms

Vatican II Documents

OT   *Optatam Totius* (Decree on the Training of Priests), 1965
PO   *Presbyterorum Ordinis* (Decree on the Ministry and Life
        of Priests), 1965
LG   *Lumen Gentium* (Dogmatic Constitution on the Church), 1964

Additional Documents

PDV   *Pastores Dabo Vobis* (Post-Synodal Apostolic Exhortation on the
        Formation of Priests in the Circumstances of the Present
        Day), 1992
EG   *Evangelii Gaudium* (The Joy of the Gospel; Apostolic
        Exhortation on Evangelization), 2013
PPF   *Program of Priestly Formation* (issued by the bishops of the
        United States), 1971, 1976, 1981, 1992, and 2005

Organizations

USCCB   United States Conference of Catholic Bishops
NCEA   National Catholic Educational Association,
        Seminary Department
ATS   Association of Theological Schools
CARA   Center for Applied Research in the Apostolate

Explanation of Terms

Theologates is the term used for major seminaries and schools of theology.
Generally diocesan theologates are called seminaries and religious order

Introduction

The Second Vatican Council closed over fifty years ago. Its official documents have had a profound impact on the life of the church, including one of the last, *Optatam Totius* (Decree on the Training of Priests). Issued on October 28, 1965, four hundred years after the Council of Trent's document on priestly formation, this new document was revolutionary and required numerous adjustments in seminaries. The main question for this book, then, is "How well have seminaries and schools of theology responded to the intentions of Vatican II?" The answer is multifaceted and measures of success are not exact, but examining the programs and practices that prepare students for ministry offers an important source of understanding. While seminarians are the primary focus of the book, lay students have been enrolling in theologates since the 1980s. Since all graduates are important to parishes, dioceses, and other church organizations, the book takes into account the experience of lay students as well.

Determining if the promise of Vatican II is being fulfilled through seminary formation programs is a demanding and urgent task because of the impact pastoral leaders have on the life of the church. The following chapters contribute to that task by exploring how and how well theologates are forming seminarians and lay ministers so that they can effectively accomplish their ministries. Various sources of information guide this effort. Of fundamental import are the five editions of the *Program of Priestly Formation (PPF)*, issued in 1971, 1976, 1981, 1992, and 2005 by the United States Conference of Catholic Bishops (USCCB). These documents have provided the authoritative guidelines for seminary formation, and each edition reflects the changing considerations of Vatican II and its influence on the way theologates organize themselves. The book refers as well to other universal and local church documents helping to shape the content and programs in theologates.

Another valuable source of information comes from the reams of statistical data gathered and analyzed by the Center for Applied Research in the Apostolate (CARA). Since 1967 CARA has surveyed seminaries annually about their status, enrollment numbers, student characteristics, and many other topics. Especially in recent years, the staff of CARA has authored comprehensive analyses of the data. Finally, for over three decades I have collected and studied information about how theologates function and have interviewed hundreds of seminary administrators, faculty, and students about their knowledge and experience of formation. Rectors/presidents have enabled me to make nearly five hundred visits to their schools to gather information and report on the findings. The data generated by these visits are important in themselves, but cumulatively they help clarify the ethos of each theologate.

Other agencies, leaders, and researchers also have been of great assistance as sources of influence and information. One of the most important organizations involving seminaries was the National Catholic Educational Association (NCEA) Seminary Department established in 1898 as the "Education Conference of Catholic Seminary Faculties." Disbanded in 2014, the Seminary Department provided critical leadership in the development of the church's theologates, gathering seminary leaders for mutual learning and disseminating information pertinent to the profession. The Seminary Department served as a liaison with the bishops' conference and established connections with foundations and donors, the Association of Theological Schools (ATS), and other organizations important to the excellence of ministerial education. The annual NCEA convention brought together faculty and administrators to hear about current practices and new research and to meet with peers to discuss interests of mutual concern. For generations the Seminary Department published research and commentary, culminating in the substantive quarterly, *The Seminary Journal*. In recent years, collaboration between the executive director of the Seminary Department, Msgr. Jeremiah McCarthy, and the head of USCCB's Secretariat of Clergy, Consecrated Life and Vocations, Msgr. W. Shawn McKnight, resulted in projects related to celibacy, liturgy and spirituality, catechesis, evangelization, ecumenism, and justice and equality.[1] They also

---

[1] CARA reports prepared for the Secretariat of Clergy, Consecrated Life and Vocations of the USCCB: *Celibacy Formation and New Faculty Formation in the Program of Priestly Formation* by Mary Gautier and Thomas Gaunt, 2015; *Liturgical and Spiritual Formation in Seminary Programs* by Mary Gautier, Thomas Gaunt, and Jonathon

arranged conferences for seminary leaders and priests, initiated research projects, and organized regular meetings of rectors/presidents.[2] For many years the executive directors of the NCEA Seminary Department were instrumental in acquiring grants to support its activities. The Religion Division of the Lilly Endowment was the major funder for many of the Seminary Department's initiatives, some of which were in collaboration with the ATS.

Membership in ATS has provided excellent support for the distinctive needs of Catholic theologates while making available to other denominations the wisdom of their Catholic counterparts in the areas of human and spiritual formation. The current executive director, Daniel Aleshire, is especially attentive to leadership development that addresses the needs of rectors/presidents, academic deans, faculty members, and other administrators. Msgr. McCarthy commented on the value of the Association with special attention to accreditation:

> ATS accreditation provides schools with a regular, ongoing opportunity for assessment of strengths and areas in need of improvement. The evidence that is gathered is based on data and established performance indicators of achievement. The information in the self-study document prepared by each school provides a historical record of a school's growth and a means of ongoing accountability to the community that it serves. For bishops and vocation directors, this data provides direct, objective evidence of a seminary's quality and its implementation of the *Program of Priestly Formation*.[3]

Wiggins, 2014; *Formation in Catechesis and Evangelization and Ecumenical and Inter-religious Relations in Seminary Programs* by Mary Gautier and Mark Gray, 2013; and *Justice and Equality: Formation in Catholic Social Teaching and Intercultural Competency in Seminary Programs,* by Mary Gautier and Joseph O'Hara, 2012.

[2] Among the projects were: *An Assessment Workbook* by Jeremiah McCarthy and Mark Latcovich, 2014, the purpose of which was to examine the tasks of assessing seminary student outcomes and seminary degree programs; The Parresia Project, led by Richard Henning, which involved faculty and others who explored ways to help prepare priests coming from other countries to minister in the US, and the communities they will serve; and a gathering of experts on "Intercultural Competencies: A Necessary Conversation" with the American Psychological Association, 2012.

[3] Msgr. Jeremiah McCarthy, former director of accreditation for ATS, served as a member of the advisory committee for this project and authored these comments concerning ATS.

Msgr. McCarthy goes on to note that ATS is a superb example of ecumenism in action. It is an agency that strengthens Catholic identity and enhances the quality of formation of priests, deacons, and lay ministers for service to the church. It helps to sustain seminaries as they deal with new and emerging challenges, ranging from the increasing diversity of students to economic sustainability, and helping seminary leaders and faculty members respond to the changing landscape of religious life in North America.

Based on these resources, the book delves into all aspects of seminary formation from the recent past through the present and on to future directions. The initial chapter examines the effects of Vatican II as it evolved since the first edition of the *PPF*. The next chapters examine the organization and personnel of the current thirty-nine theologates in the United States by considering the mission, vision, and structure of each, as well as their leadership of boards, administrators, and faculty. Research on students and programs constitute the next several chapters. The numbers and characteristics of both seminarians and lay students who are preparing for ministry are studied, with reference to the significant difference in their backgrounds and attitudes from many of the Catholics they will serve. With this profile in place, the book turns to the nature of the programs in human, spiritual, intellectual, and pastoral formation that will influence the sort of pastoral services the graduates will provide. The final chapter suggests new directions that seem appropriate and necessary in the preparation of seminarians and lay ecclesial ministry students if the people of God are to be served well.

The book concludes with commentaries by five seminary leaders who also served on an advisory committee for the book project. The issues, related to their expertise, are on the spirituality of leadership by Rev. Ronald Rolheiser, OMI, president, Oblate School of Theology; the significance of generational differences in the church by Dr. Thomas Walters, dean emeritus, Saint Meinrad Seminary; human formation by Rev. Leon Hutton, dean of Human Formation, St. John's Seminary, Camarillo, California (now pastor); trends in Scripture study and preaching by Sr. Barbara Reid, OP, vice president and academic dean, Catholic Theological Union; and the culture of encounter in seminary formation by Msgr. Peter Vaccari, rector, St. Joseph's Seminary and College, Dunwoodie in Yonkers, New York.

The overall findings point to a sharper focus on priestly ministry than thirty years ago in the mission and vision statements of diocesan theologates, especially those that are operated by dioceses rather than religious orders. While lay students continue to be enrolled in relatively high numbers, many of these schools have created programs for them separated from seminarians. Religious order theologates usually have more unified programs. The leadership of theologates has undergone rapid change in the past decade. Board membership has expanded significantly to include more people with financial expertise. The terms of rectors/presidents are shorter than at any other time in the past thirty years with about 75 percent in their first five years of office. Their role identity is determined in part by their attention to internal or external responsibilities, and these vary in relation to their understanding of the mission. Duplicate structures for seminarians and lay students, as well as the initiation of new degree and certificate programs, have added financial strain on some schools. Institutional development staff and activities increased to respond to new financial requirements. Faculty composition shows a significant decline in the proportion of priests, dropping by 20 percent since 1985, and an increase of 15 percent of laypeople. At the same time, priests on faculty are now expected to accept increased responsibilities for human formation advising and spiritual direction. Retirement of longtime faculty reached a high point in the past decade. All of this signals a new era of seminary leadership.

The most noteworthy change for seminarians is the human formation program, a new addition as a separate program in response to the directives of Pope John Paul II in *Pastores Dabo Vobis* (*PDV*) issued in 1992. Field experiences in pastoral settings are more diverse, but these do not always match the changing demographics of church members.

Recently, fifty years after the council, Pope Francis opened the Holy Door of St. Peter's Basilica to inaugurate the Jubilee Year of Mercy. In his opening homily, the pope remembered the Second Vatican Council as "a genuine encounter between the Church and the men and women of our time."

> Wherever there are people, the Church is called to reach out to them and to bring the joy of the Gospel, and the mercy and forgiveness of God. After these decades, we again take up this missionary drive with the same power and enthusiasm. The Jubilee challenges us to this openness, and demands that we not neglect the spirit which emerged from Vatican II, the spirit of the Samaritan, as Blessed Paul VI expressed it at the conclusion of the Council.[4]

[4] Francis, homily, Holy Mass and Opening of the Holy Door, Extraordinary Jubilee of Mercy, December 8, 2015, http://w2.vatican.va/content/francesco/en/homilies /2015/documents/papa-francesco_20151208_giubileo-omelia-apertura.html.

It is these sentiments of encounter and openness that need to define the purpose and inspiration of preparation for ministry. In *Evangelii Gaudium* (*EG*; The Joy of the Gospel) and in many of his addresses, Pope Francis elaborates on what ministry should be like. He speaks of cultural challenges (61–67) such as secularism, individualism, and globalization that affect our ability to inculturate the faith (68–70). In the extensive pronouncement on preaching, he specifies the challenge in this way:

> Proclaiming the Gospel message to different cultures also involves proclaiming it to professional, scientific and academic circles. This means an encounter between faith, reason and the sciences with a view to developing new approaches and arguments on the issue of credibility, a creative apologetics which would encourage greater openness to the Gospel on the part of all. (*EG* 132)

Pope Francis also offers advice that would serve well the agenda for any pastoral formation program: "The preacher also needs to keep his ear to the people and to discover what it is that the faithful need to hear. A preacher has to contemplate the word, but he also has to contemplate his people . . . paying attention 'to actual people, to using their language, their signs and symbols, to answering the questions they ask'" (154). No one underestimates the challenge this poses for those charged with preparing the church's future ministers. It is a challenge to ground people in the intellectual, liturgical, and spiritual traditions of the church while encouraging the sort of human development that equips them with the fluency to "link the message of a biblical text to a human situation, to an experience which cries out for the light of God's word" (154). This book will hopefully serve as a resource to this transformative end.

Chapter 1

The Effects of Vatican II on the Present State of Seminaries and Theologates

Background and Overview

Few aspects of church life have been affected as profoundly by the Second Vatican Council as the theological schools where men are prepared for priesthood, and especially in the past twenty-five years where laypeople study to become lay ecclesial ministers.[1] While many theologians and other commentators have analyzed the impact of Vatican II on the church as a whole, it is only more recently that several authors have taken up in a substantial way how the work of the council related to priestly formation.[2] Until the 1970s most seminaries closely resembled those prescribed by the Council of Trent's 1563 Decree on Seminaries. Leaders made few substantial changes until several years after Vatican II, though by the mid-1960s some authors began writing about needed modifications and

---

[1] The term "theological schools" or "theologates" refers to diocesan seminaries and religious order schools of theology. Diocesan seminaries commonly enroll religious order candidates as well, and both types of schools also often enroll some lay students. The change in the numbers of schools and students is shown on the chart in appendix 1-A.

[2] The most thorough treatment of the topic is by Maryanne Confoy, *Religious Life and Priesthood: Perfectae Caritatis, Optatam Totius, Presbyterorum Ordinis* (Mahwah, NJ: Paulist Press, 2008).

a few models incorporated adaptations in design and method. To most Catholics, even past the mid-twentieth century, these institutions seemed enclosed and impenetrable. Much of what had transpired in seminaries for four hundred years changed radically in 1965 with the publication of *Optatam Totius* (OT), the Vatican II Decree on the Training of Priests.[3] That document continues to influence seminaries and pastoral formation programs for both seminarians and lay students.

The chapter provides a short historical background on priestly formation, with brief comments on the role and character of seminaries through the centuries. In the second section, attention turns to what *OT* says, how it is understood, and its enormous impact on seminary formation. Then follows a discussion of the *Program of Priestly Formation (PPF)*, mandated for each country by *OT* and published five times in the United States between 1971 and 2005. Theological schools adapted their formational and educational programs with each succeeding edition, with a declining emphasis on the teachings of Vatican II in later editions. The final section of the chapter seeks to uncover possible reasons for the evolution in thinking about and the practices of pastoral formation since Vatican II, especially over the past thirty years. These developments can best be understood by considering the bishops who served on the committees that authored the *PPF*s through the years, such as their backgrounds and involvement with Vatican II. It also describes the role of faculty by assessing how changes in the approaches to and content of curriculum from the early 1980s to the present were affected by the council.

A. History of Seminaries

The long history of priestly formation has passed through many phases. In fact, the three years Jesus spent with his chosen Twelve is sometimes referred to as the first "seminary program," complete with all four "pillars" as found in the current *PPF*, namely, human, spiritual, intellectual, and pastoral formation. For the first four centuries, no formal program or institutions for the education of seminarians has been uncovered. During Augustine's time, the local synod in Carthage "called for a priestly training that produces priests 'who know scripture, can preach, understand church

---

[3] The translation used for Vatican II documents is Austin Flannery, ed., *Vatican Council II: Constitutions, Decrees, Declarations; The Basic Sixteen Documents* (Collegeville, MN: Liturgical Press, 2014).

laws and are upright in their personal behavior.'"[4] Even then the majority of priestly formation was done in the form of apprenticeships with local bishops or parish priests, while students stayed in their family homes.[5]

From the seventh to the thirteenth centuries priestly formation gradually began to take shape in the form of episcopal (cathedral) and monastic schools, but a comprehensive history of seminaries is not available for this early period.[6] From 1123 to 1215 four of the five Lateran ecumenical councils met at the Lateran Cathedral in Rome and, among other topics, they dealt with aspects of clerical life. One result of the third Lateran Council in 1179 was a mandate that a priest be appointed to the cathedral and that he be responsible and remunerated for the formation of local clerics. The fourth Lateran Council of 1215 further required that this priest be a theologian who would teach the Scriptures and pastoral theology.[7]

In the twelfth and thirteenth centuries, seeds of present formation structures were sown in university programs, for example, in Paris, Bologna, and Rome. The programs were available for both religious and diocesan candidates for the priesthood, but most likely few parish priests were trained in these schools, especially if they were destined for the countryside. Rather the schools were established for "elite ministers for high society."[8] In response to "the sorry moral condition of the clergy," residential life with a rigid regimen was established, including compulsory devotions and "demanding asceticism."[9] Nonetheless, with these few exceptions, "during the years preceding the Protestant Reformation, clerical formation in general lacked a solid and well-balanced intellectual and moral foundation and a practical preparation for ministry."[10] In the period after the establishment of university programs and before the Council

---

[4] Confoy, *Religious Life and Priesthood*, 77–78. Reference to Christopher M. Bellitto, "Priestly Training before Trent: Rethinking Some Evidence from the Long Middle Ages," in *Medieval Education*, ed. Ronald B. Begley and Joseph W. Koterski (New York: Fordham University Press, 2005), 35–49.

[5] Ibid., 78.

[6] Ibid., 77–78.

[7] Michael Papesh, *Clerical Culture: Contradiction and Transformation* (Collegeville, MN: Liturgical Press, 2004), 62.

[8] Confoy, *Religious Life and Priesthood*, 78.

[9] Joseph White, *The Diocesan Seminary in the United States: A History from the 1780s to the Present* (Notre Dame, IN: University of Notre Dame Press, 1989), 2; and Confoy, *Religious Life and Priesthood*, 78.

[10] Confoy, *Religious Life and Priesthood*, 79.

of Trent, several developments influenced the direction of formation for priesthood, especially in 1552 in Rome when the Jesuits opened their Collegium Germanicum and in late 1555 in England.[11]

Over a period of nearly twenty years (1545 to 1563), the Council of Trent addressed many issues related to the clergy. In an early session of the council (1546) a decision was made that colleges should be established solely for priestly training in every diocese (c. 16, final version c. 18). It was a decision that would have reverberating effects for many generations. "It is difficult to exaggerate the canon's long-range influence."[12] These schools "sought to isolate and protect priestly candidates from the dangers of the world, to educate and form priests who would serve the church and keep their parishioners away from the aberrations of the era. The intention of the entire Tridentine Decree on Seminaries was to protect 'endangered youth' by removing them from the world and to fortify them in their priestly vocation."[13] In its twenty-third session, in July 1563 the Council of Trent issued its Decree on Seminaries. This decree "represented a major change in seminary training in terms of its reform of the diverse and inconsistent types of formation for ordination that had prevailed globally over the centuries."[14] Since bishops were assigned responsibility for determining how their candidates were to be formed morally and intellectually, different forms of clerical training resulted from diocese to diocese. Nonetheless, the decree founded the seminary system as it substantially existed at the time of the opening of Vatican II.

The Council of Trent decree indicated that "the theological and ascetical training for diocesan priests was based on the model of the risen Christ as priest and victim. The emphasis on priestly vocation that prevailed in this model was less that of service to the people than of an inner call to life in Christ. The monastic approach to priestly vocation and formation influenced much of the writing on the spirituality of the diocesan priest even until Vatican II."[15] On academic formation, the decree stated that the seminarians "should study grammar, singing, keeping church accounts and other useful skills; and they should be versed in Holy Scripture, church

---

[11] John W. O'Malley, *Trent: What Happened at the Council* (Cambridge, MA: Harvard University Press, 2013), 212.

[12] Ibid.

[13] Confoy, *Religious Life and Priesthood*, 79.

[14] Ibid., 78–79.

[15] Ibid., 80.

documents [*libros ecclesiasticos*], homilies of the Fathers [*sancti*], and the practice of rites and ceremonies and of administering the sacraments, particularly all that seems appropriate for hearing confessions."[16] At the time, the council did not intend that every priest be educated to the same level, but all were expected to live an upright life.[17] Those living in rural areas and dioceses had fewer opportunities for study, while those in cities had available a form of the cathedral schools of the past.

Response to Trent's Decree on Seminaries was rapid. In 1565, Pius IV established the Roman College, attached to the Roman Seminary, as a Tridentine model for all dioceses.[18] Within a few years, the number of lay students enrolled in its classes far exceeded that of clerical candidates so that by 1639 some 130 lay students were enrolled along with 40 clerical students. "By the seventeenth century, the formation and spirituality of the diocesan seminary was fundamentally shaped by the French model of the Sulpicians and Vincentians."[19] Later other religious orders developed their own seminaries; the Benedictines and Jesuits in particular were strongly influential.

Great disparity was evident in the way dioceses implemented the requirements set out by the Council of Trent. Even well into the twentieth century considerable variation could be found in the quality of priestly formation programs and in the ways they were implemented. The same might be said for the twenty-first century.

B. Development of *Optatam Totius*

The council fathers of Vatican II developed *OT* with a clear understanding of how the training of priests should be intimately intertwined with the pastoral life of the church, and so they paid close attention to *Presbyterorum Ordinis* (*PO* [Decree on the Ministry and Life of Priests]), already approved by the council. Cardinal Leo Joseph Suenens captured

---

[16] O'Malley, *Trent*, 214.

[17] Ibid., 213.

[18] Confoy, *Religious Life and Priesthood*, 79–80.

[19] Ibid., 80. Both Sulpicians and Vincentians conducted many seminaries in the United States through the years, the Sulpicians first beginning in 1791 and the Vincentians from 1818 onward. Vincentians tended to emphasize mission experiences and pastoral formation and Sulpicians tended to have a stronger intellectual tradition. Sulpician formation also called for the directors and faculty to live together with the seminarians on a one-to-one approach of formation.

this necessary connection when he said, "Vatican Council II must create a new kind of seminary in line with the needs of today."[20] Not all of the council fathers were in agreement as some argued for faithfulness to past seminary training and processes. It was the divergence of opinion between adaptation to changing circumstances and adherence to tradition that was the basis of the bishops' discussions on seminary training during the drafting of the decree. These disparities illustrate how strongly the different sides felt about the shifts, and it also reveals some of the compromises the council fathers made to reach the level of consensus required by Paul VI. Nonetheless, the schema was passed with a vote of 2,074 for and 41 opposed. *OT* underwent some elaboration and reordering and was finally passed on October 28, 1965, receiving a nearly unanimous vote.[21]

What Is the Content of *Optatam Totius?*

From the first paragraph onward considerable disagreement is evidenced between the traditional and the progressive council fathers about the direction *OT* should take. In the introduction, the document first acknowledges the "supreme importance of priestly formation" and in the same sentence goes on to assure the more traditional bishops that it would strengthen the regulations that had long been in use and shown to be sound. At the same time it promises those who see the need for a new kind of seminary that it has added new elements that "correspond with the constitutions and decrees of this council and with the changed conditions of our time" (*OT* Introduction). The prescriptions of the decree directly concerned the training of diocesan clergy, but were to be appropriately adapted to all clerical training, including religious and monastic priests.

Areas of emphasis in *Optatam Totius*

1. Development of priestly formation programs tailored to the needs and circumstances of the region. Each episcopal conference was to undertake programs that responded to the particular circumstances and pastoral needs of the region. This decentralization displeased some of those in the Curia who were used to a uniform program for formation of priests over

---

[20] Ibid., 77.
[21] John W. O'Malley, *What Happened at Vatican II* (Cambridge, MA: Harvard University Press, 2008), 240.

which they had control, but the call for inculturation and respect for local churches was already embedded in the thinking of other commissions and so curial opposition did not prevail. This mandate appealed to the bishops and, in John O'Malley's words, "It was also symptomatic of the council's consistent concern for adaptation to local circumstances and for placing more discretion into local hands."[22]

2. *Importance of fostering vocations.* During its preliminary work, the commission responsible for *OT* expressed great concern about the significant decline in vocations that was already occurring. While very little debate took place because of the high level of agreement about the content of the section of the document on "More Active Encouragement of Priestly Vocations," several bishops spoke to its importance due to the "crisis of vocations" in many parts of the world, especially in Europe. They ascribed the problem to "the de-Christianization of the world (especially the Western world), the smaller size of Catholic families, and the failure of church leaders to encourage vocations."[23] Thus the tendency to blame the actions of Vatican II for the decline of vocations did not hold for Europe since the pattern of diminishment happened before Vatican II; in the United States, the considerable drop in vocations came so soon after the end of the council—already by 1969 it was 6,602, a decrease of almost 25 percent from the beginning of the council—that the decline would erroneously be attributed as a direct result of the council (see appendix 1-A). The significant decline by 1970 in enrollment in high school seminaries was perhaps more likely related to the council, which exhibited a lack of enthusiasm for this level of formation. While the high school system, much more in use in parts of Europe than in the rest of the world, was accepted, it was not imposed in *OT*. Instead, the decree emphasized the role of the family in developing vocations.

3. *Centrality of pastoral training, thus breaking from the isolation of seminary life.* At the heart of the decree is section III on setting up major seminaries. The preliminary discussion sets the tone by expressing a widely

---

[22] Ibid. Although this was the first time such a directive was given, the issuance of the *Ratio Fundamentalis Institutionis Sacerdotalis* by the Sacred Congregation for Education in 1970 contributed to a more common approach throughout the world.

[23] Confoy, *Religious Life and Priesthood*, 83: Bishop Kieran Conry in Ireland "was astounded to discover that one group of Catholics ascribed the loss of priestly vocations and all the ills of the church, 'including, inexplicably, the horror of clerical child abuse, to the Second Vatican Council.'" From *Priest & People* (August 2003).

supported position that the decree needed to be systematically tied to *PO* and the document that would become *Lumen Gentium (LG)*. Speaking on behalf of the commission preparing the Decree on Seminaries, Giuseppe Carraro, bishop of Verona, named "the five characteristics of the schema: its pastoral dimension, adaptation to the present day, adaptation to the needs of different localities and peoples, balanced synthesis, and appropriate renewal. Pastoral concern, he said, informed all the propositions and he hoped they would promote an 'organic and vital synthesis' in the education of priests."[24] Later at least three other elements were added, calling for "a more pastoral approach to the process of formation, for a deeper biblical formation, and for more adequate methods of education."[25]

Furthermore, this section sets out the ends toward which all formation is to be oriented. Priests are to be prepared for (1) the ministry of the word, so that they understand the revealed word of God, meditate on it, and express it in words and in example; (2) the ministry of worship and sanctification, so that through their prayers and sacred liturgical celebrations they might perfect the work of sanctification; and (3) the ministry of the parish, so that they might know how to make Christ present as they give their lives in service having become servants of all, that they might win over all the more. The summary affirms the direction: "All aspects of their training, therefore—spiritual, intellectual and disciplinary—are to be coordinated by joint action with this pastoral purpose" (*OT* 4). This section introduces what is often referred to as the "servant model" of priesthood, starkly contrasted with the "cultic model" of recent years.

In this section, the document also identifies the desirable characteristics of faculty: they should be prepared in sound doctrine, suitable pastoral experience, and special spiritual and pedagogical training. Administrators, under the rector's leadership, are to form a closely knit community. Admission of candidates is to be done with "watchful concern" with only those who are worthy of being promoted and others given direction to embrace the lay apostolate.

4. Spiritual training, including celibacy. The primary emphasis of *OT* is found in the fourth section, "Greater Attention to Spiritual Training." It begins with the admonition that "spiritual formation should be closely

---

[24] Giuseppe Alberigo and Joseph A. Komonchak, eds., *The History of Vatican II, Vol. 4: Church as Communion: Third Period and Intersession, September 1964–September 1965* (Maryknoll, NY: Orbis Press, 2003), 357.

[25] Ibid., footnote 115.

allied to doctrinal and pastoral training" and that all aspects of formation should be integrated. Seminarians are to be taught to seek Christ, meditate on Christ, and imitate Christ, "especially the holy Eucharist and the Divine Office. Let them seek him too in the person of the bishop who sends them and in the people to whom they are sent, especially the poor, the little ones, the sick, sinners and unbelievers." Practices of piety are commended, "but care must be taken that spiritual formation not be reduced to pious exercises alone nor merely develop religious sentiment" (*OT* 8).

Reinforcing the concept of the servant model, seminarians are to be made fully aware of the burdens they are undertaking. The document affirms that they should be admonished to give their lives with a generous heart and to "realize that they are not destined for a life of power and honors, but are destined to be totally dedicated to the service of God and pastoral ministry" (*OT* 9). Very little is said about celibacy except that students are to be educated in the tradition of celibacy and are to see it as "a gift to which, inspired by the holy Spirit and helped by divine grace, they must freely and generously respond." Aided by suitable safeguards, "they are to be warned of the dangers their chastity will encounter" (10). Other admonitions are put forward: the norms of Christian education are to be observed, formation is to be complemented by findings of sound psychology and pedagogy, so as to be able to make sound decisions and develop human maturity. "But the discipline is to be applied in such a way that the students make it their own, so that they accept the authority of superiors from inner conviction and for reasons of conscience," that is, for supernatural reasons (11). Toward these goals, "the bishops must set aside a suitable period of time for more intensive spiritual training" (12).

5. *Connecting philosophical and theological studies with the modern world.* The fifth section of *OT*, "The Revision of Ecclesiastical Studies," is considered second in importance only to spiritual formation. It provides a thorough discussion of the place of philosophical and theological disciplines as essential elements of priestly formation. Regarding philosophy, the text states that students should "take account of modern philosophical developments" and that "subjects should be taught in such a way that students are first of all gradually led to a solid and coherent knowledge of human nature, the world and God, guided by the philosophical tradition of lasting value . . . so that with a proper understanding of the present age, they will be equipped for dialogue with people of their time." It continues, "Careful attention should be paid to the close connection between philosophy and the real problems of life" (*OT* 15). Notable is the absence

of specific mention of Thomas Aquinas in the discussion of philosophical disciplines, but later, under theological disciplines, he is mentioned briefly: "Then, in order to throw the fullest light possible on the mysteries of salvation, let them learn through speculation guided by St. Thomas to enter into them more deeply and see how they are interconnected, to recognize how they are present and active in liturgical celebration and in the whole life of the church" (16).[26]

Also in this section, *OT* underscores the central role of the study of the Bible. In addition to careful initiation into the method of exegesis, daily reading of and meditation on the Bible for inspiration and nourishment is encouraged. Dogmatic theology is to be arranged in order to deal with biblical themes first and then with the general history of the church. It is at this point that St. Thomas is mentioned, as noted above. The decree identifies several other specific theological areas to be studied: moral theology, canon law, and church history. "Liturgy, which is to be regarded as the first and ever necessary source of true Christian spirit, should be taught in the spirit of articles 15 and 16 of the Constitution on the Sacred Liturgy" (*OT* 16). Students also are to be given a fuller understanding of other Christian churches and ecclesial communities, as well as of other religions. The final paragraphs insist that "teaching methods need to be revised," excessive multiplication of courses is to be avoided, and those who serve in seminaries are to be well trained and suitable in "character, virtue and talent" (17, 18).

6. *Pastoral training.* This section on "Strictly Pastoral Training" reflects the insistence in *OT* that pastoral concern is to permeate thoroughly the entire training of the students so that they are prepared for catechesis and preaching, administration of the sacraments, works of charity, and other pastoral functions. Formators are to develop certain qualities in students, "such as the ability to listen to others and to open their hearts in a spirit of charity to the various kinds of human need" (*OT* 19). This pastoral development is to take place during the course of studies and in summers.

7. *Ongoing formation.* The final section of the document focuses on younger priests who "can be gradually introduced to priestly life and apostolic activity from the spiritual, intellectual and pastoral point of

---

[26] In the 1970 *Ratio Fundamentalis Institutionis Sacerdotalis*, slightly more is said of the role of St. Thomas. Both documents emphasize the necessity of integrating philosophy and theology.

view, and thus renew and develop this life and activity" (*OT* 22). As they conclude *OT*, the bishops note that Vatican II pursued the work begun by the Council of Trent. Seminary faculty and administrators have responsibility for forming future priests and those preparing must realize that "the hopes of the church and the salvation of souls are being committed to them" (Conclusion).

How important was *OT*? Many commentators believe it represented an almost total overhaul of the entire system for the training of priests; others saw it as mainly adjusting what had lasted for an extended period of time, since the Council of Trent. The former view seems more accurate in light of the changes that were to appear in theological schools, especially in the succeeding decades.

C. Development of Programs in Theological Schools— 1971 to the Present

Considering how theological programs developed after Vatican II, it is obvious that the themes of *OT* served as a significant guidepost in creating the first edition of the *PPF* and its revisions in 1976 and 1981. Its powerful impact on seminary formation continued until Pope John Paul II issued his *Pastores Dabo Vobis* (*PDV*) in 1992, an exhortation that shifted the primacy of place held by *OT* from the years of 1971 to 1991. The changes can be measured in several ways, such as by analyzing the points of focus, the overall content of the documents, and the prevalence of quotes from each of the documents in the respective editions. The explanation for why the shifts occurred is complex, but several indicators help explain the changes. One element is the difference in how each committee of bishops understood what the council called for as they wrote and revised the *PPF*. Another factor is the change in theological school faculties as they responded to the bishops' directives and incorporated the teachings of Vatican II in adapting their formational and educational programs from 1971 to the present.

References to Vatican II in the *Programs of Priestly Formation,* 1971 to 2005

In determining both the immediate and lasting influence of Vatican II on theological education in seminaries, it is instructive to note the references made to Vatican II documents in successive editions of *PPF* in

1971, 1976, 1981, 1992, and 2005. The study shows a declining number of quotations from and references to the council from the first to the fifth editions (see table 1.1).

Table 1.1

References to Vatican II in the Five Editions of the Program of Priestly Formation

Document	1st	2nd	3rd	4th	5th
Optatam Totius (Decree on the Training of Priests)	40	47	43	13	15
Lumen Gentium (Dogmatic Constitution on the Church)	10	11	6	15	4
Presbyterorum Ordinis (Decree on the Ministry and Life of Priests)	4	4	3	19	10
All Other References to Documents (# of other documents used)	24 (8)	29 (8)	16 (6)	7 (6)	9 (7)
Total	**78**	**91**	**68**	**54**	**38**
General References to Vatican II	26	40	36	13	15
Grand Total	**104**	**131**	**104**	**67**	**53**

The First Three Editions, 1971, 1976, and 1981. The first edition of the *PPF* was published in 1971, just six years after the close of the council. Already then the authors incorporated the thinking represented in the documents of Vatican II, with 104 references, 78 to specific documents, many of them quoted at length. In addition, they made 26 general references, often with the point of establishing how important the council was in the development of the first *PPF*. As expected, the most frequently used document was *OT* (Decree on the Training of Priests) and second was *LG* (Dogmatic Constitution on the Church). In 1971, *Unitatis Redintegratio* (Decree on Ecumenism) was third, surpassed later by *PO*. Eight other documents were mentioned 1 to 4 times (see appendix 1-B for details).

The second edition, published in 1976, reached a peak in its focus on Vatican II. It added 27 more references for a total of 131, with 91 of them to specific documents. Again the top two, *OT* and *LG*, remained the same. Perhaps somewhat curiously, the third most frequently quoted document was *Christus Dominus* (Decree on the Pastoral Office of Bishops in the Church). Eight other documents were mentioned from 1 to 5 times for a total of 25. *Unitatis Redintegratio* dropped to fourth place.

By the time of the third edition, published in 1981, fifteen years after the close of the council, the number of references to Vatican II documents dropped to 104 (the same number as in 1971), with 68 references to specific documents. *OT* was the only one frequently mentioned; though again in second place, *LG* dropped from 11 to 6 references; seven other documents were mentioned from 1 to 4 times for a total of 19. The council documents were still quoted more frequently by far than any other source.

The Last Two Editions, 1992 and 2005, and the Influence of Pastores Dabo Vobis. The two most recent editions of the *PPF* showed a dramatically changed pattern in their use of Vatican II documents. More than ten years passed between the third and fourth editions, the former issued in 1981 and the latter in 1992, twenty-six years after the close of the council. The total number of references to Vatican II dropped from more than 100 in the three previous editions, to 67 in the fourth edition, with 54 relating to specific documents. Three major changes were notable. *PO*, mentioned only 3 or 4 times in the first three editions, was now in first place with 19 references. Again in second place, *LG* was referenced 15 times. Most dramatically, *OT*, until now in first place with 40 or more references in each of the three previous editions, was reduced to only 13 references, suggesting that this decree was no longer the primary guiding document for seminaries. Six other documents were mentioned only once or twice for a total of 7 times, illustrating the reduced impact of Vatican II in comparison with previous editions. Replacing the Vatican II documents were 85 references to *PDV*.

The fifth edition of the *PPF* published in 2005, forty years after the end of the council, includes the fewest references to the council at 53, with 38 referring to documents. The latter number is less than half of the 91 references at its peak in 1976. *OT* returned to first place, but with only 15 references; second with 10 references was *PO*. *LG* was reduced to 4 from 15; the other six documents mentioned were referenced once or twice for a total of 9 times. Again, *PDV* is quoted or referenced 76 times, more often than all the conciliar documents, and in those instances occasional secondary references are made to a Vatican II document. Yet, *PDV* is only second in number of quotes in 2005. Codex Iuris Canonici (Code of Canon Law, 1983) was referenced more than 90 times, the latter paralleled by Codex Canonum Ecclesiarum Orientalium (Code of Canons of Eastern Churches, 1990). By comparison, in 1992, references to the Code of Canon Law numbered only 23 and were not mentioned at all in earlier editions (see appendix 1-C).

The shift in emphasis clearly moved from Vatican II references to *PDV* and the Code of Canon Law. The foreword to the 2005 *PPF* states that this edition was influenced by consultation with bishops, major superiors, and seminary rectors with others in their administrations and that it was "also greatly influenced by the Apostolic Exhortation of John Paul II, *Pastores Dabo Vobis* (1992)." The authors make no mention of Vatican II in the foreword. In the preface the primary role of *PDV* is reiterated in the first paragraph; the second paragraph refers to *OT* and footnotes three other Vatican II documents: *Lumen Gentium*, *Christus Dominus*, and *Presbyterorum Ordinis*. The introduction quotes John Paul II's *Novo Millennio Ineunte* (At the Close of the Great Jubilee of the Year 2000), which stated that the council itself was "the great grace bestowed on the Church in the twentieth century." Generally, references to Vatican II in the fifth edition of the *PPF* quote a few words or make broad statements related to the council, in contrast to extended quotations in earlier editions.

Responses of Seminaries to the Directives in *Optatam Totius*

The intentions of the council fathers regarding priestly formation were clearly communicated in *OT*. Almost immediately following the end of the council, and in some cases even during the council, seminaries made adjustments to their programs and methods of education. Some seminary leaders responded with changes in the early years, as recorded in histories of seminaries and in articles from that period.

During the years of the council and even earlier in the 1950s, the reformation of seminary life was a topic of frequent discussion among seminary administrators and faculty. A number of articles by seminary educators were published in journals read mostly by priests, but as soon as the council ended, several volumes and many articles were available for a much wider audience.[27] A common theme of this first phase was

---

[27] See especially James Keller and Richard Armstrong, eds., *Apostolic Renewal in the Seminary in the Light of Vatican II: The Program of Priestly Formation* (New York:

the criticism that seminarians were too isolated and thus not prepared for engagement in ministry when they finished their studies and were ordained. Some authors, notably Stafford Poole, a Vincentian, suggested that "if the seminary is to keep abreast of the modern world, it is going to have to be reunited organically with lay education."[28] He believed that seminary reform was the key to the church's renewal.

In what might be considered a second phase, these changes were reinforced with the publication of the first two editions of the *PPF* in 1971 and 1976 for seminaries in the United States. In them, the bishops' committee wholeheartedly embraced the major themes of the council and, quoting frequently from its documents, enjoined seminary leaders to change their institutions to conform to the new patterns. In the third phase, the dependence on and mentions of the work of the council diminished gradually in the 1981 edition of the *PPF* and markedly, as noted above, in the fourth and fifth editions (1992 and 2005), when *PDV* and the Code of Canon Law became the chief guiding documents.

In *Vatican II: The Battle for Meaning*, Massimo Faggioli reinforces this pattern of evolution: "The fidelity of mainstream Catholic theology to Vatican II meant rather undramatic work for university and seminary teachers who from 1966 onward transformed their courses on sacramental theology, on ecclesiology, and on anthropology."[29] However, he adds that their work did not prevent difficulties in the process of the reception of the council's documents, and "in opposition to the moderate and reformists attitude embodied by Paul VI, the questioning of the legitimacy of Vatican II created the first real discontinuity in the reception of a general council in the second millennium." He continues, "Even if the traditionalist movement became more and more radical in the late 1970s and the 1980s, extreme opposition to the council did not wait a decade at the end of Vatican II to disavow it."[30] The seeds of doubt about the council were

---

Christophers, 1965); James Michael Lee and Louis J. Putz, eds., *Seminary Education in a Time of Change* (Notre Dame, IN: Fides, 1965); and Stafford Poole, *Seminary in Crisis* (New York: Herder and Herder, 1965); also, for a later analysis of the influence of Vatican II see T. Howland Sanks, SJ, "Education for Ministry since Vatican II," *Theological Studies* 45 (September 1984): 481–500.

[28] Poole, *Seminary in Crisis*, 14, 28–29; also as quoted in White, *The Diocesan Seminary in the United States*, 413.

[29] Massimo Faggioli, *Vatican II: The Battle for Meaning* (New York: Paulist Press, 2012), 23.

[30] Ibid., 24.

sprouting and growing, as is reflected later in seminaries as well as in the exercise of pastoral ministry by many recently ordained priests.

A variety of sources confirmed the readiness of seminaries to receive the mandates of the council in the twenty to thirty years following the end of the council. Faculties implemented the teachings of the council in all aspects of programs, from spiritual formation to curriculum, from community life to pastoral experience. Yet, as is now evident in many situations, that receptivity and implementation has moderated, if not diminished, through the years.

In what ways were the major points of *OT* and other Vatican II documents reflected in the first *PPF?* And how did the response change from the first to the fifth editions? At the outset, the US bishops established that their authority to write and promulgate a document on seminary formation came explicitly from *OT* as one of its first mandates. It stated that it was the responsibility of each nation and region to develop its own program of priestly formation, which was to be revised from time to time and approved by the Apostolic See. The US bishops conformed to this directive by issuing the first *PPF* in 1971; others followed in 1976, 1981, 1992, and the fifth edition in 2005.[31] *OT* was the major source for the first *PPF*, along with the *Ratio Fundamentalis Institutionis Sacerdotalis.*[32] As each succeeding edition of the *PPF* was modified, the use of *OT* as the foundational Vatican II document on seminaries shifted. Following are several examples of changes related to both content and method.

The pastoral dimension was the framework for all aspects of the formation program according to *OT.* In the first edition of the *PPF*, the authors emphasized the relationship between belief and life, which was to be actualized in theological method that helped students develop logical rigor to bring experience and reflection into their studies. "Pastoral concern resounds throughout the Decree on Priestly Formation," according to the first *PPF*, and it "'ought to permeate thoroughly the entire training of the students,'"

---

[31] The sixth program of priestly formation was scheduled to be published in 2015, but was delayed in part because of changes in the organization of the Roman Curia. The expected date of publication is now 2020.

[32] *Ratio Fundamentalis Institutionis Sacerdotalis* (A Basic Scheme for Priestly Training), developed by the Congregation for Education for use by the bishops' conferences to assist them in formulating their own programs (1970, rev. 1985), sets out the fundamental norms for the formation of future priests. The Congregation said that the purpose of the document was "to preserve unity and at the same time allow sound variety."

a sentiment reflected throughout the document (*PPF* I 94, quoting *OT* 19). Toward that end the authors included a lengthy section on field education, a relatively new concept in seminary training at the time. By 2005, many other more pressing issues had intervened, especially those arising from the sexual abuse crisis, so the urgency of pastoral ministry education was somewhat diminished when the fifth edition of the *PPF* was published. The goal of pastoral formation was said to be "the formation of a 'true shepherd' who teaches, sanctifies, and governs or leads," but in the same paragraph it states, "It is important not to sacrifice human, spiritual, and intellectual formation for practical experience" (*PPF* V 239). The message of the divergent statements indicates a shift in attitude: pastoral education is viewed as necessary, but it should not take precedence over other areas of formation. This caution echoes the attitude of the small number of council fathers who did not approve of widening the scope of seminary formation.

Sacred Scripture was highlighted in *OT* and in the first *PPF*, where it quoted at length from *Dei Verbum* (Dogmatic Constitution on Divine Revelation) and made note of its significant role as the basis for academic and spiritual formation. The accompanying narrative indicated that "the central task of the Scripture professor is exegesis of the sacred text so that the student may have the best possible understanding of the sense intended by the sacred authors" (*PPF* I 51). The first *PPF* also underscored the importance of students learning the historical-critical method as an essential tool for exegesis. "The course in Sacred Scripture should serve to initiate the student in biblical criticism, contribute to his understanding of the message of the entire Scriptures, and provide a significant exercise in biblical criticism of particular parts" (*PPF* I 53). In the fifth *PPF* the most significant shift was the comment regarding the historical-critical method: "The proper understanding of Sacred Scripture requires the use of the historical-critical method, though this method is not totally sufficient" (*PPF* V 200). The previous emphases in *OT* and the first *PPF* was not as evident in the last *PPF*.

The third example has to do with methodology. The first *PPF* states that students should be able to evaluate the strengths and limitations of past and current theological speculation, noting that a student "should learn how to use biblical and historical sources in his theological thinking and how to relate this thinking to his personal faith, life, and apostolate" (*PPF* I 60). Further, the document affirms that the plurality of theologies "should be accepted and encouraged" for a deeper understanding of our common faith (*PPF* I 34). A separate section under Methodology, labeled "Pluralism," gives attention to the place of Thomas Aquinas. This paragraph makes reference to *OT* and reflects the compromise reached among the council fathers about the role Aquinas was to be accorded. *Ratio Fundamentalis Institutionis Sacerdotalis* (A Basic Scheme for Priestly Training) maintains that students "should regard St. Thomas as one of the Church's greatest teachers while still esteeming authors of more recent times" (86, 1970). As noted above, specific mention of Thomas Aquinas is absent in the discussion of philosophical disciplines in *OT*, but under theological disciplines his place is strongly asserted (OT and footnote 36). In the most recent *PPF*, the importance of Aquinas is reiterated (*PPF* V 157 and footnote 102).

Particularly strong in *OT* is the call for integration of academic, pastoral, and spiritual formation. In the first *PPF* this admonition was clearly reflected, with many references to ways of presenting the program so that seminarians would learn to provide spiritual leadership and achieve a greater degree of personal and emotional maturity for the sake of ministry. An underlying goal was to attain a sense of personal responsibility. While no specific section is dedicated to human formation, elements of that dimension are identified in later editions and touched on in the three major components of formation identified above, along with community life.

Through the intervening years and until now seminaries have held fast to the goal of integration and it is considered a foundational approach to the implementation of priestly formation. However, the goal of comprehensive integration is yet to be achieved to the extent directed in *OT*: "In the revision of ecclesiastical studies, the primary aim is to coordinate philosophy and theology in such a way that together they open the minds of the students more and more to the mystery of Christ, which touches the whole of human history, continually influences the church, and is at work particularly in priestly ministry" (14).[33] A substantial section of *OT* called for philosophy to be taught with the goal of relating studies so that they were connected with the modern world, pastoral training, and breaking from the isolation of seminary life. Numerous conversations about how to establish a meaningful relationship between philosophy and theology and other aspects of the program have occupied faculty through the years, but has yet to be achieved.

---

[33] See *LG*, nn. 7 and 28.

The following list indicates the disposition of major changes emphasized in *OT*:

1. The *pastoral dimension* was to be the framework for all aspects of formation according to *OT.* In the 2005 *PPF*, pastoral education is viewed as necessary, but it is not to take precedence over other areas of formation.

2. *Sacred Scripture* was highlighted in *OT* and was to be the basis for academic and spiritual formation. In the 2005 *PPF*, the previous emphases are present, though the importance of the historical-critical method is lessened.

3. Concerning *methodology*, the primary aim of *OT* was to make a connection between philosophy and theology and the real problems of life. It affirmed that the plurality of theologies "should be accepted and encouraged" for a deeper understanding of our faith. In the 2005 *PPF*, greater emphasis is given to Thomas Aquinas, while other theologians should be considered.

4. *OT* calls for *integration* of academic, pastoral, and spiritual formation, a goal still considered foundational to the implementation of priestly formation, though not yet fully achieved.

D. Change in the Use of Vatican II Documents in the *Program of Priestly Formation* and in Theological Schools

Shifts in interpretation of the role Vatican II should play in seminary formation have occurred in many areas. Data on the use of the council's documents in the *PPF*s from 1971 to 2005 show a pattern that is in some ways predictable and in other ways unexpected. Seeds of doubt about its interpretation had been planted. Moreover, in 1992, before the issuance of the fourth edition of the *PPF*, Pope John Paul II had written *PDV*, which incorporated many of the same topics contained in *OT* and then became a major reference point for the last two editions. The rise and fall in the number of references is perhaps not so surprising for two other reasons—changes in bishops who authored the various editions of the *PPF* and changes in faculty teaching in seminaries.

Changes in Bishops

By the time the fourth and fifth editions were published, the bishops who were responsible for developing the texts for the most part had not experienced Vatican II in person; thus, twenty-six years after the council (1992, the date of the fourth edition) or forty years after (2005, the date of the fifth edition), the council's impact and influence had lessened. The ages of the bishops at the beginning of the council who served on the *PPF* drafting committees are revealing: their average age *in 1962* ranged from forty-nine for the authors of the first edition to sixteen for authors of the fifth edition (see appendix 1-D). Obviously, committee members' experience of the council differed widely and no doubt affected their identification with the thinking of the council fathers. Of the twenty-three committee members for the 1971 edition of the *PPF*, all sixteen who were bishops by 1965 attended the council, fourteen of them attended all four sessions, along with a fifteenth priest who served as a *peritus* and later became a bishop. Of the six committee members who did not attend the council, five were made bishops after the council ended and one was an elderly bishop unable to attend.

The second edition was staffed by three bishops who attended the council and ten who did not attend; all were ordained as priests before the council. No one who worked on the third or fourth edition attended Vatican II. No one in the youngest group staffing the fifth edition was yet ordained as a bishop—or even as a priest—in 1962 and just a few were old enough to be in college and fewer still in theological studies. Personal familiarity with the council likely played a role in decisions to incorporate more or less of its teachings in the various editions of the *PPF* for which they were responsible.

Besides direct participation in the council and being of age during the council, the popes who appointed each set of bishops may add to the explanation for their stronger allegiance either to Vatican II documents or to *PDV* (see appendix 1-E). Four different popes ordained those bishops serving as members of the committee for the first edition—from Pius XI to Paul VI. Only five years later Paul VI ordained all but one of the second edition committee members, and in 1981, after five more years, all were ordained by Paul VI. By 1992, when the fourth edition was published, six were ordained by John Paul II and only two by Paul VI. Finally, in 2005, all eleven members were ordained by John Paul II. As expected, this pattern corresponds to the age of bishops as Vatican II commenced. Even by the third edition in 1981, the composition of the bishops had changed substantially; by 2005 the change was all-embracing.

Changes in Seminary Faculty

In the 1980s the number of seminary faculty averaged around 900. Of these, only 51 were still teaching full time in 2014–15—30 religious priests, 6 diocesan priests, 8 laymen, 5 laywomen, 1 sister, and 1 brother. Most of them are likely to be in their late sixties or early seventies, representing the small remaining group of those who were young adults during the council. Those 51 faculty equal 6 percent of all faculty, few of whom are teaching in diocesan seminaries. It is possible that a small number of older faculty who were not teaching in the early 1980s but are over sixty-five are among the 871 still teaching full time.

At the same time, the many recently hired faculty teaching full time in seminaries earned their graduate degrees while studying with faculty who themselves were born after 1960, removing the experience of the council another step away from those who experienced the council as young adults. This configuration makes difficult the task that Richard Gaillardetz and Catherine Clifford see as an essential role for seminary faculty. They say that teachers must assist students/seminarians in understanding what "fuller participation of the laity" means and how to celebrate in a meaningful way for today's congregations. The seminary faculty needs to encourage seminarians and other students to explore the meaning of fuller participation of the laity in the Eucharist, as well as participation on councils and committees using their expertise. The task of seminaries is to help seminarians flesh out what all this might mean for a pastor.[34]

E. References to Vatican II in Theological School Catalogs— Early 1980s to the Present

Whatever the disposition of faculty, references to Vatican II in seminary catalogs have actually increased over the period of time from the early 1980s to the present from 205 to 252 (in the 35 schools with comparable information available). Possibly these numbers have minimal significance since on average the number of references grew from about 6 per school to just over 7 (see appendix 1-F). Most of the references are found in course descriptions, of which there were 166 in the 1980s and 213 in the 2010s. Another 39 references in each of the decades were distributed in other

---

[34] Richard Gaillardetz and Catherine Clifford, *Keys to the Council: Unlocking the Teaching of Vatican II* (Collegeville, MN: Liturgical Press, 2012), 79.

areas, including the history and purpose of the schools and in reference to formation programs (see appendix 1-G). Besides the numbers, from specific examples such as the liturgy and ecumenism, very different outcomes result depending on the method of incorporating Vatican II thinking.

Concerning the liturgy, *OT* 16 stresses the centrality of the liturgy and urges that it should be taught according to the viewpoint of *Sacrosanctum Concilium* (Constitution on the Sacred Liturgy). The first *PPF* quotes extensively from this constitution: "The study of Sacred Liturgy is to be ranked among the compulsory and major courses in seminaries and religious houses of studies; in theological faculties it is to rank among the principal courses" (*PPF* I 69, quoting *Sacrosanctum Concilium* 16). It advises that the liturgy should be intimately linked to spiritual and pastoral formation. In the fifth edition of the *PPF*, *Sacrosanctum Concilium* is mentioned only in one footnote and that is in reference to celibacy. The directives about teaching the liturgy indicate that it should be included in the core, related to other areas of formation, and celebrated "according to the mind of the Church, without addition or subtraction" (*PPF* V 214).

The place of liturgy is not elevated to the same degree in the latest *PPF*. However, a 2009 study on the state of liturgy in seminaries yielded very positive findings from the forty-seven faculty who teach courses on liturgy.[35] To the statement, "*Sacrosanctum Concilium* is the basis of our liturgical formation program," 96 percent agreed (66 percent agreed strongly and 30 percent agreed) and 4 percent were undecided. Overall the faculty were at least moderately satisfied with the content and method of teaching liturgy and the implementation of liturgical celebrations. Other questions and the narrative responses yielded mixed results. For example, when asked if seminarians in our school were overly concerned about rubrics used in liturgy, 34 percent of the faculty surveyed agreed, 17 percent were undecided, and half disagreed. On the negative side, in the narrative more than half the comments (13 of 23) concerned the rigidity and stiffness in liturgical celebrations in seminaries. All in all, the survey suggested that the teachings of *Sacrosanctum Concilium* are being followed in teaching, but not as strongly in the understanding of students or in liturgical practices.

Concerning ecumenism, the final chapter of the 1971 *PPF* is devoted entirely to the "Ecumenical Dimension of Theological Education" in

[35] Study by Katarina Schuth, conducted for the annual meeting of the Federation of Diocesan Liturgical Commissions, 2009. The study was done before the recent English translation of the Roman Missal went into effect.

formation at the theology level. It quotes several passages from *Unitatis Redintegratio* (Decree on Ecumenism) and details its relationship to spiritual, academic, and pastoral formation. The concluding section lists a number of concrete actions to be undertaken in implementing an ecumenical program, including cooperation with non-Catholic seminaries.

The fifth edition of the *PPF* touches only briefly on the topic of ecumenism in six places, three having to do with academic studies, two with pastoral application, and one with spiritual formation. On the topic of theological curriculum (*PPF* V 163), it states that theology studied in a seminary should contribute to the mission of the church by being concerned with Christian unity, and so the studies must impart adequate grasp of the Catholic principles on ecumenism (here they are referring to the Decree on Ecumenism). Later it states that the core should include a course on ecumenism and "[it] should be fully integrated into other courses, thus permeating the theological curriculum. Issues concerning interreligious dialogue also should be discussed" (*PPF* V 216). Another citation concerns the faculty who are to teach about the beliefs and practices of other churches or religions; they may be members of those churches or religions, but seminarians should have taken ecclesiology and ecumenism courses beforehand so as to have a more informed understanding of ecumenical relations (*PPF* V 224).

The two references to ecumenism dealing with pastoral formation are concerned with interaction with other churches and religions. In the first instance, the focus is on learning how to interact with different churches: "Religious pluralism: they also need to know, appreciate and learn how to work within the ecumenical and interfaith context that forms the backdrop for life in the United States and for the Catholic Church in this nation" (*PPF* V 239). The second pastoral recommendation concerns the experiences seminarians should have. When they are ecumenical in nature, they must be respectful of Catholic teaching, especially on moral and ethical issues, and the sacramental dimension of pastoral care must be integral to such programs. Clinical Pastoral Education is given as an example of an opportunity for engaging in ecumenism, both with other participants and in the hospital setting. This opportunity was mentioned in the first edition of the *PPF*, and in the next three editions, it is encouraged. In the fifth edition it is listed merely as one of many possibilities and is not specifically identified as the official Clinical Pastoral Education program, but rather a clinical experience. In recent years the number of seminaries requiring CPE has declined considerably, from twenty-four requiring it in 2000 to only eight requiring it presently. This shift is viewed by many faculty as a significant loss of an occasion for ecumenical encounter.

Other ways of shifting the importance of ecumenism can be identified. For example, while the fifth *PPF* specifies that ecumenism is to be a core course, only seven of thirty-nine theological schools actually require it. Five others combine it with ecclesiology or missiology in their course titles, and perhaps others include some aspects of ecumenism, but they do not mention it. The *Instrumentum Laboris* for the Apostolic Visitation of the Seminaries and Houses of Priestly Formation in the United States in 2005 mentioned numerous documents as sources, among them the "Directory for the Application of Principles and Norms on Ecumenism,"[36] but the final report of the Congregation for Catholic Education, December 2008, makes no mention of ecumenism. In recent years the topic has not been emphasized by those responsible for developing the norms for seminary curricula.

Conclusion

The transformation in seminary formation is linked closely to the understanding and experience of Vatican II. With each subsequent edition of the *PPF*, authors and contributors to these documents were less and less personally connected to the council, including the bishops on the committees and the faculty who teach in these seminaries. The open question is whether they will be able to or strongly desire to continue the tradition of Vatican II established in *OT* and *PO*. This concern is more than a matter of being for or against Vatican II. The teachings of the council were meant to expand the vision of the church's self-understanding in how it proclaims the Gospel and engages the world in its own transformation. In a sense, how the insights of the council continue to influence the preparation of seminarians and others for pastoral service should be a matter of urgent concern. As new generations of priests assume their responsibilities, the approaches they employ in the exercise of ministry become unmistakable signposts of the church's boldness in its mission. Clerical leadership is singular in its power to shape the life of the Christian community and to engage the wisdom and commitment of lay ecclesial ministers and parishioners. The following chapters will explain in detail the evolution of theological education, with special attention to the past thirty years.

---

[36] Pontifical Council for Promoting Christian Unity (1993), see especially 192–95.

PART II

Organization and Personnel

Chapter 2

Mission, Vision, and Structures

A. The Mission and Vision of Theologates

Expressions of Mission

The mission statements of the thirty-nine theologates enrolling seminarians in 2015 are for the most part based on three important documents: *Optatam Totius* (Vatican II Decree on the Training of Priests, 1965), *Pastores Dabo Vobis* (pastoral letter of Pope John Paul II, 1992), and *Program of Priestly Formation*, fifth edition, 2005. While the mission statements of theologates share some common features, they also vary considerably depending on their history and founding mission, educational purposes and types of students, location, and other factors. Of the schools studied here, thirty were established for diocesan seminarians and nine others for religious order seminarians. Since their founding almost all have broadened the scope of their missions. All but four mission statements indicate that lay students preparing for ecclesial ministry may enroll, along with priests, religious, and, in some cases, deacons. Many diocesan schools now enroll religious order seminarians, but only rarely do religious order schools enroll diocesan students.[1] A few diocesan schools enroll only a small number of

---

[1] Of the thirty theologates established for diocesan seminarians, thirteen enrolled ten or more religious candidates in 2015 (CUA had the highest number at fifty-seven), twelve enrolled fewer than ten religious candidates, and five enrolled no religious order candidates. The nine theologates established for religious order candidates seldom enroll diocesan seminarians, but all enroll lay students.

lay students, but in some cases they enroll numbers equal to or larger than the number of seminarians.[2] In the latter cases, lay programs are usually designed specifically for lay students, and offered in one of two ways: as an integral part of the program with seminarians or, in four instances, as totally separate programs under the auspices of the seminary.

Mission statements often begin with a primary emphasis on preparing candidates for ordination to the priesthood. Phrases nuance this emphasis, such as "according to the mind of Jesus Christ" or "configured to Christ" or "in the image of Christ the Good Shepherd." Most diocesan seminaries list the four areas of formation—human, spiritual, intellectual, and pastoral—required by the *PPF*. Religious candidates usually receive human and spiritual formation in their respective communities rather than in the religious-sponsored theologate they attend for academic work. In delineating the purpose of formation, diocesan and religious schools use some common and some unique expressions. Both understand the purpose to be that of preparing priests for service in the kingdom of God, ministering to God's people, being responsive to the contemporary needs of the church, and serving as priests in the Roman Catholic Church.

Diocesan seminaries focus on parish ministry, how to pastor communities of the faithful, leadership in parishes, and priestly service in the diocese. Schools for religious candidates often express the purpose of their programs more broadly in terms of the church's mission and ministry in the world. They embrace varied and broad contexts such as promoting ecumenism and interreligious dialogue, engaging faith and culture, and, in a few cases, being explicit about advancing theology through scholarly contributions. Several identify their mission in relation to their religious order's special charisms, such as preaching, monastic apostolates, missionary service, or promotion of justice and reconciliation.

Most theologates identify a secondary mission by listing others whom their programs serve, typically persons preparing for lay ministry. Some schools explicitly name their intent to reflect the collaborative nature of ministries today, to offer opportunities for professional pastoral preparation for those serving church and society, or to provide a theological foundation for men and women desiring to pursue doctoral studies. The degrees of-

---

[2] Of the thirty diocesan theologates, twenty-six mission statements state that they admit lay students and thirteen of them enrolled more than twenty-five lay students. Of the nine religious order theologates, lay students are included in all mission statements and in 2015 they enrolled at least twenty-five lay students.

fered to lay students include the master of divinity, but more typically lay students enroll in two-year master of arts in various theological or pastoral fields. In recent years about one-fourth of lay students were enrolled in certificate programs, while three-fourths pursued a degree. In addition to these offerings, several schools have a commitment to formation for the diaconate. In 2015, just over four hundred of the two thousand deacon candidates were enrolled in ten diocesan theologates, most often in separate programs.[3] Priests, religious, and others attend theologates for advanced degrees and continuing education, but enrollment in the latter programs has declined sharply in recent years, due in part to fewer diocesan priests being granted sabbatical time and the enormous drop in the number of women religious.

Thirteen schools—six diocesan and seven religious—do not differentiate or designate any one group as being their primary constituency but rather include all potential enrollees in a single inclusive mission. This finds expression in various ways: commitment to preparing men and women for academic and apostolic vocations; formation of leaders of competence, conscience, and compassion; preparation of men and women to serve the church as scholars and teachers; and preparation of professional ministers for service in the Roman Catholic Church, for the purpose of evangelization, or for the diverse ministries represented in the student body. A few diocesan schools in this category mention candidates for the priesthood first, but all types of students are identified in a single sentence that speaks to their providing education and formation for priestly ministry as well as lay ministries. The contrasting ways of expressing mission is indicative of the diversity that shows itself in almost every aspect of the way theologates operate.

Even as the mission of many theologates has evolved, resulting in a greater variety of students, the 2005 *PPF* and the 2008 Vatican Visitation report dampened the momentum of the late 1980s to educate seminarians and lay students in a more collaborative environment. Theologates are now more likely to underscore their primary purpose of preparing men for priestly ministry. They often issue separate catalogs and other publications for each group, and in some places integration of students is prohibited.

---

[3] The ten programs are but a fraction of the 166 programs that prepare men for ordination to the diaconate, as reported by CARA, but they enroll 20 percent of the deacon candidates.

Yet, other theologates, most notably those operated by religious orders, continue to follow their commitment to and belief in collaborative preparation for ministry. The more expansive mission statements are supported by enrollment of students whose vocations represent lay and ordained, and by new programs that accommodate the wider range of students.

Expressions of Vision

In conjunction with the mission statement, the vision expands on the ways each school accomplishes the mission and elaborates on its purposes in light of ecclesial and student needs. In the past, the vision often identified the geographic focus of the theologate to serve the population of a specific regional location in the United States or presented a more comprehensive view, that is, to deepen the global vision of the church. In the past twenty years, the intercultural nature of theologates grew immeasurably, as evidenced in the composition of faculty, staff, and students and in learning opportunities available in degree programs and in experiences in other cultures and countries. Ideally, this vision impacts a pastoral orientation that involves practical and reflective engagement with the multicultural global reality of the church and society.

Other vision statements speak of far-reaching program goals, such as standing on the cutting edge of the dialogue between the Gospel and human culture and welcoming newcomers to the United States. Adopting this wider perspective often results in attracting a more diverse student body. A similar vision sought to provide resources for the wider church by promoting vocations and offering continuing education for clergy and laity coming from a variety of backgrounds and cultures. More specific topics are mentioned: commitment to social justice, dedication to the new evangelization, or attentiveness to the teachings of Vatican II. Shortly after the close of the council, many schools emphasized interfaith and ecumenical dialogue and exchange. Though some still incorporate this dimension in their vision, many others now devote less attention to it.

A third approach to grounding mission in vision is to identify the character of educational outcomes. Vision statements incorporate a wide variety of expressions to describe their concept of effective pastoral ministers: for example, modeling and living out servant leadership, becoming builders of communion in church and society, modeling and fostering collaboration in ministry, or meeting the church's needs, expectations, and ideas about ministry in evolving circumstances. Most vision statements recognize the need for pastoral adaptation to the twenty-first century in order to meet the needs of the contemporary church with its diverse cultures.

B. The Structures of Theologates

Structural models of theologates vary in several ways, based on their sponsorship and operation, on who attends, and on their relationship with other Catholic higher education institutions (see appendix 2-A). In many instances the sponsors and those who operate the theologates are the same entity, but others have varied arrangements:

- diocesan-owned and -operated theologates—fifteen (thirteen arch-diocesan and two diocesan; one archdiocese sponsors two seminaries, the second is for older seminarians);

- diocesan theologates owned and operated by religious orders—seven (three Benedictine [OSB], one each Society of Saint Sulpice [SS], Society of the Missionaries of the Holy Apostles [MSsA], Oblates of Mary Immaculate [OMI], and Priests of the Sacred Heart [SCJ], all of which also may enroll their own and other religious order seminarians);

- religious order-owned and -operated for religious—nine (three Dominican, two Jesuit, one Franciscan, one Holy Cross, one Bene-dictine, and one multiple orders); and

- other arrangements—eight (four owned by corporations; three owned by bishops, one owned by an archdiocese and operated by the Sulpicians).

A second way of categorizing theologates is on the basis of who may be admitted as students. Occasionally students are enrolled even though the theologate does not list their participation as part of its mission. In effect, twenty-five of thirty diocesan schools admit lay students, but in some cases lay students do not attend classes with seminarians. Students in religious order schools generally attend classes together. Considering all thirty-nine theologates, enrollment is as follows:

- sixteen admit diocesan and religious priesthood candidates and lay students;

- five admit diocesan and religious priesthood candidates, with sepa-rate programs for lay students;

- four admit diocesan priesthood candidates and lay students;
- four admit diocesan and religious priesthood candidates only;
- one admits only diocesan priesthood candidates; and
- all nine religious order theologates admit religious priesthood candidates and lay students and one of them also enrolls two diocesan students.

A third structural dimension concerns relationships of theologates with other Catholic higher education institutions. In the past decade fewer and fewer theologates are totally self-contained and now almost 40 percent are significantly involved with other institutions and many others have lesser agreements. Nine theologates are an integral part of a university where most students live on or very near the campus. Six have their own institutional identity, but collaborate in some way with a university, and/or their students attend a university but live in a different location. These relationships augment resources for theologates and provide expanded opportunities for students. In other cases, even when formal arrangements are not part of the structure, students may cross-register or participate in other activities at a nearby university or a seminary of a different denomination. Many theologates are part of ecumenical or interfaith consortia and other less formal relationships, though interest and activity in this area has waned in recent years.

This analysis of structures highlights the complexity of theologates and demonstrates the diversity of sponsorship, operation, students, and relationships with other institutions. The breadth of these affiliations and connections may not be readily understood as an advantage by some students, but the dialogue among students of different backgrounds and with different vocational calls enriches the formational experience.

Outcomes of Mission, Vision, and Structural Changes

Since the mid-1980s, the focus of theologates shifted, as witnessed in modifications in mission and vision statements. The adjustments came about principally as a result of directives in *PPF* V and in the report of the Apostolic Visitation of American seminaries in 2008, both of which stressed the importance of reinforcing priestly identity. The *PPF* speaks only of seminarians studying in theologates and makes no mention of lay students. It specifies that formation departments are to be headed by priests and that faculty in Sacred Scripture and dogmatic theology should be priests. However, it does encourage collaboration with laity who teach in other areas and who work in other church ministries. The Apostolic Visitation report states that a "clear distinction between the common priesthood and the ministerial, hierarchical priesthood needs to be emphasized more" and it cautions that "problems can also arise when the seminary aims at offering a theological education to all—seminarians and laity—for, unless proper safeguards are put in place, the seminary can lose much of its finality, which is to offer a specifically *priestly* formation to men, chosen by the Church to embark on the path to Holy Orders."[4]

The content and tone of these church documents gives little recognition or encouragement for the presence of lay students in theologates, although most enroll from as few as twenty-five lay students to as many as several hundred. In most diocesan seminaries, the focus on seminarians is more clear-cut and lay students are disconnected from them. This change is reflected in separate catalogs and/or website presentations of programs and courses and, different from most religious order schools, the clearly secondary place accorded lay ministry education in the mission statement. The different expressions of the vision of theologates further distinguishes them, with a growing divide between most religious order schools and diocesan schools, which are also distinguished by their sponsorship and their involvement with religious orders. The less frequent meeting of theologate leaders and faculty is in part responsible for the differentiation.

Mission and vision statements bring together the essence of what a school espouses. While those statements in the thirty-nine theologates studied here tend to be clear and unambiguous, they nonetheless reveal a continuing uneasiness, especially for diocesan schools, about how best to prepare both priesthood candidates and those lay men and women seeking formation for ministry. At the core of this unexpressed dilemma is the often underdeveloped opportunity to create environments in which the distinctive needs and vocational outlooks of seminarians and lay students can become a powerful resource for the formation of priests and the formation of women and men who will serve alongside them in the critical work of proclaiming the Good News.

[4] Congregation for Catholic Education, Report on the Apostolic Visitation of American seminaries, December 15, 2008, "II. General Conclusions of the Apostolic Visitation," Section 1, 5.

Chapter 3

Leadership
Boards, Administration, and Faculty

Introduction

Leadership in theologates is shared among governing boards, administrators, and faculty. Each group makes distinct contributions to effective management, but all share the goal of creating an institution that provides the best possible formation for seminarian and, in most settings, lay ecclesial students. The quality of relationships between boards and key administrators often determines the degree of success of the school. Where faculty also share in this relationship by serving on board committees and meeting with board members, the depth of knowledge and understanding enhance the quality of the education. The structure, membership, and responsibilities of each group is described in this chapter.[1]

A. Governing Boards

Introduction

Governing boards began to play a role in the life of theologates only in the mid-to-late 1960s. By the mid-1980s, their roles had expanded and membership numbers and expertise had grown significantly. Since then boards have become major assets in providing counsel, advocacy, and encouragement to many theologate leaders. Although thirteen fewer theologates were operating in 2015 than in 1985, the number of board

---

[1] See commentary by Ron Rolheiser, "Toward a Spirituality of Ecclesial Leadership."

members has grown by almost a hundred. Not all boards function at the same level, however, and their roles vary considerably depending on the structure of the board, the level of preparation for the role, interaction with administrators and faculty, and the leadership of board chairs and rectors/presidents. In these institutions board dependence on the rectors/presidents is critical since they must be able to present the mission of the theologate as a worthwhile endeavor to attract prospective members. It is the obligation of the rectors/presidents to inform members about challenges and needs so that they feel their expertise is valued.

Structure and Membership

The structure of boards, the way they function, and their membership vary considerably. Besides the quality of leadership of rectors/presidents, the differences stem from their status as freestanding, university-related, or collaborative, and from their sponsorship by dioceses or religious orders. Of the thirty-nine theologates, twenty-five have one governing board, ten of them have two, two have three, and two others—whose students attend university-related theology departments—do not have a separate board though they usually have a committee related to the university board. In total, fifty-one boards performing various governing functions are active. They hold at least ten different titles, including eight boards of corporate members, comprised entirely of those in charge of the dioceses and religious orders that sponsor the theologate. Of the other forty-three boards, the most frequently used title is board of trustees (25); next is board of directors (7); board of overseers follows (4); boards of regents, advisors, and governors have two each (6); and there is one board for ecclesiastical faculty (1). When a theologate has two or three boards, the additional ones are usually small corporate boards or secondary boards comprised mainly of laity who serve in an advisory capacity.

Almost always the local ordinary serves as chair of the board, that is, a cardinal, archbishop, or bishop for diocesan schools and a religious priest for religious order schools. In five theologates, a layperson is chair of the board and in one a religious brother. Nonetheless, canon law prescribes that ultimate authority rests with the local ordinary. A total of 907 people served on theologate boards, some of whom served on more than one board and are thus counted twice (see table 3.1). The average size of boards is eighteen, virtually identical for all types of theologates. Yet individual boards range in size from eleven to forty-four, apart from corporate boards that are as small as four. Nearly half the members (48.6 percent) are bishops or priests, and most of the remaining members are lay men and women (44.1 percent); deacons, women religious, and religious brothers make up 7.3 percent, and a few are not identified by vocation.

Table 3.1

Changes in Governing Board Membership, 1985–2015

	1985		2015		Change	
Board Member	Number	Percent	Number	Percent	Number	Percent
Cardinals/bishops	98	12.0	144	15.9	+46	+3.9
Diocesan priests	157	19.1	114	12.6	-43	-6.5
Men religious	278	33.9	182	20.1	-96	-13.8
Women religious	30	3.7	22	2.4	-8	-1.3
Laymen	188	22.9	263	29.0	+75	+6.1
Laywomen	60	7.3	137	15.1	+77	+7.8
Other	9	1.1	21	2.3	+12	+1.2
Not identified	--	--	24	2.6	+24	+2.6
TOTAL	820	100.0	907	100.0	+87	

During the past thirty years, lay members of boards have increased by 13.9 percent and cardinals and bishops by 3.9 percent, even as diocesan priests have decreased by 6.5 percent and religious priests by 13.8 percent. The increase in the number of laity can be attributed to greater participation of laity in church activities generally and to the need for their particular expertise, especially in financial matters. The increase in the number of cardinals and bishops is often related to perceived advantages in recruiting seminarians from their dioceses. The decline in the number of men religious can be accounted for largely because they operate fewer theologates and supply fewer faculty to theologates overall. The reason for the decline in the number of diocesan priests is less obvious, but perhaps it is related to making room for more laypeople and members of the hierarchy.

Board Functions and Responsibilities

Most boards responsible for the ordinary governance of theologates meet three times a year to keep informed about recent developments and make decisions on major policies and issues. In some situations meetings take place over a day or more, involve extensive committee activity, and include board education; others meet briefly and infrequently, and without much opportunity for participation at meetings. Typically, corporate boards meet less often and only as prescribed in the bylaws; boards of advisors and overseers meet once or twice a year and provide broader perspectives. Between meetings, CEOs are personally in touch with at least some of the board members, usually the executive committee. Several university-related theologates have committees related to the university board of which they are a part, or at least they report to the larger board.

Depending on the location of board members, committees meet with varying frequency, in person or by electronic means. Typically boards make use of four or five committees, such as finance, advancement, formation, and board affairs. From the beginning, assistance with fiduciary matters has been a central function of boards and continues to be crucial during recent times of financial constriction; as a result, a higher proportion of laypeople with financial expertise populate boards. All members receive communication about ongoing activities on a regular basis. If a theologate has more than one board, coordination among them is essential to their proper functioning.

The bylaws of each school define the responsibilities of boards, but the extent of participation of board members is not limited to these areas and is usually broader. The recent survey of rectors/presidents identified the many ways in which boards served their schools.[2] Not surprisingly, topics related to expertise on finances topped the list of what they used and valued most, followed by advice on mission, vision, and planning, including assistance with recruitment and public relations. These leaders also appreciated the overall assessment and evaluation provided by the boards, especially when it was accompanied by personal support and encouragement. Notable is the similarity of topics identified as important by current rectors/presidents when compared with their counterparts of two decades ago.

Related to finances, the rectors/presidents said they were assisted most significantly by advice on fundraising and development, such as creative ways to expand the donor base, find other sources of funding, and hire

---

[2] Of the thirty-nine rectors/presidents, 87 percent responded to a lengthy survey, which covered board functions and a wide range of other topics.

staff with specific expertise needed by the school. Advice on investment strategies, ways to solidify their holdings, and institute proper budgeting procedures were also useful. One rector remarked, "Our board offers valuable advice on financial management and other operational matters such as establishing an appropriate budget and working on expanding our development initiatives." Some also mentioned the importance of active participation of board members in institutional advancement through financial contributions.

Related to mission, vision, and planning, rectors/presidents said the boards not only allowed them to gain and maintain a broad perspective, but they helped keep the strategic plan on track. In developing plans leading to more effective formation programs, boards provided a clear vision of the direction the theologates should be taking, generated new ideas, and shared standard practices for academic institutions, and also made and supported decisions. One rector observed, "They make exceptional recommendations. They see themselves involved in the mission, and their enthusiasm for it has helped me maintain mine, which in turn, flows into the faculty and student body." To ensure a successful future, board assistance with public relations has added to the favorable image of many theologates and has often resulted in recruitment of more students.

The third category of comments by rectors/presidents about their interaction with boards involved a "two-edged sword," that is, assessment and evaluation on one hand and personal support and encouragement on the other. Some boards regularly appraised the competence of administrators and articulated the strengths and weaknesses of programs. At their best, boards are willing to address difficult issues concerning the ongoing life of the theologate while providing important moral support and encouragement to leaders. Connecting appreciation for both challenge and reassurance, one rector said, "They have been particularly supportive in terms of helping us better assess our effectiveness and at the same time most encouraging of my efforts through their comments and interest in what I am doing."

When asked what additional assistance was needed from their boards, the overwhelming choice of rectors/presidents was related to financial matters, especially seeking out advice on fundraising for a variety of priorities and projects such as scholarships and renovation and construction of buildings. A strong second preference was for guidance on marketing and recruitment. Those who had served as rectors/presidents for less than five years were more likely to mention the areas where they felt they lacked background, such as in legal matters and business practices. Interestingly, only one person commented on the need for strengthening involvement of the board or improving its way of operating. Interaction between board members with faculty and other administrators was not mentioned and is often lacking, though when it does take place it can serve as a dependable means of educating board members about the school. Board development was not identified as a necessary exercise, but it would most likely be beneficial for most boards.

Summary and Analysis

It is evident from the survey, from interviews, and from other reports that the contributions of boards are highly valued and the engagement of most members is significant. It is also true that a few boards function less commendably for reasons that include being almost entirely advisory with no real authority, meeting infrequently, or making little use of the expertise of board members. However, over the past three decades, most boards have increased their effectiveness by engaging in board development efforts and becoming more knowledgeable about the mission of the institutions they serve.[3] Rectors/presidents are making better use of the expertise of the enlarged lay membership, and they are becoming more accountable to the recommendations given by them. Several respondents expressed these positive developments in different ways:

- "The board members are a wonderful blessing; they are prayerful and eager to learn."

[3] Two organizations have been decisive in assisting theologates with board development: The In Trust Center for Theological Schools identifies itself as "a membership organization that strengthens the governance and institutional capacity of theological schools, promotes their health, and facilitates their renewal through Resource Consulting, education, and publications." The Center publishes *In Trust*, "a quarterly magazine for seminary governing boards and others who bear responsibility for institutions of theological education" (see more at http://www.intrust.org/Authors/Christa-R-Klein#sthash.LH4BmhKO.dpuf; see http://www.intrust.org). The second organization, the Association of Theological Schools (ATS), "provides a host of programs, services, research, and other resources to support the work of administrators and faculty at member schools. The Commission on Accrediting of ATS accredits institutions and approves degree programs offered by accredited schools" (see http://www.ats.edu). It sponsors programs concerned with board responsibilities and requirements for accreditation of its member schools.

- "They have been particularly supportive in terms of helping us better assess our effectiveness and their moral support is a real plus."

- "The board members provide a great witness for how deeply people value priesthood by the way they promote our seminary."

The facts and views reported by current rectors/presidents bear remarkable resemblance to the results of the study of boards of all ATS accredited seminaries relative to board membership and structures, challenges and achievements.[4] Among the concerns of some respondents were the multiple responsibilities of many of their board members, resulting in little time for board education and other activities that would acquaint them with the school. An even worse situation was when members had a conflict of interest that divided their loyalties among several theologates. Generally speaking, members are more skilled in financial areas and so discussion about formation programs is of limited interest. Most boards would benefit from achieving a more balanced membership by adding members with expertise in various areas of formation. Such influences would conceivably assist rectors/presidents in focusing programs that prepare seminarians and lay students to meet the needs of the church. However, this direction is not likely to be followed since theologate leaders are quite satisfied with the present situation.

B. Administration

Introduction

Modifications in leadership structures and personnel constitute an area of substantial change in theologates since the 1980s. Rectors/presidents, for example, have shifted their emphasis from internal to external concerns, or vice versa, depending on their understanding of the mission of their schools. Even more noticeable is a sharp increase in the number of administrators. The addition of directors in academic administration and the expansion of human formation programming have altered the organization and roles of administrative personnel. In the past, it was common for one administrator to be the sole director of programs in a given

---

[4] Barbara G. Wheeler and Helen Ouellette, *Governance That Works: Effective Leadership for Theological Schools*, Auburn Studies series (New York: Auburn Theological Seminary, no. 20, March 2015).

area, but the work is now divided among two or three or more individuals in almost every aspect of formation. More complicated technological advancements have caused many schools to hire personnel to deal with internal and external uses of technology, such as publication of catalogs, recruitment materials, and online courses. Other departments, such as institutional advancement, have grown in proportion to financial need. The consequence is that among the thirty-nine theologates over a hundred different titles are used for directors with various areas of responsibility; obviously, some titles denote only slight variations for similar positions. This section provides statistical information and analysis of change dealing with categories of administrators: chief executive officers (CEOs who usually hold the title of rectors/presidents) and other major administrators, among them academic deans, vice rectors and vice presidents, as well as numerous directors and assistants for lay students, pre-theology, libraries, and facilities management.

1. Rectors/Presidents (CEOs)

Backgrounds of leaders. The chief administrators of theologates are identified by a variety of titles, reflecting the positions they fill and the roles they exercise. Most often the chief executive officers are named rector or president or some combination of the two. The titles for leaders of diocesan seminaries are most often a combination of "rector and president" (16) or simply "rector" (11); in religious order schools the term may be "president" (5) or dean. In some situations the leadership is more complicated and the CEOs have similar titles or other combinations.[5] A

---

[5] Of the many examples of variation, three diocesan seminaries associated with universities have CEOs with the titles of "rector and vice president" or "vice president and rector" or "rector/dean." Where academic functions are separate from other aspects of formation, as in four other university-related schools, the dean or chair of the theology department is the major leader for academic functions. These associated institutions are Catholic University of America and Theological College, University of Notre Dame and Moreau Seminary, Saint John's University and Saint John's School of Theology and Seminary (Collegeville), University of St. Thomas and St. Mary's Seminary (Houston). In these cases, the rector of the related seminary, not the university dean or chair, is included in this discussion. However, when analyzing intellectual formation, university deans and chairs are included. Two other religious order theologates are associated with universities, and their leaders are called deans. Since they do not have a separate institution for formation, they are included in this discussion; the seminarians live in a number of formation houses of their respective

shift in the vocational status of the leaders, a pattern also found among faculty, occurred between 1989 and 2015 from a majority of religious order priests to a majority of diocesan priests (see table 3.2). For the first time, a diocesan priest is serving as president of a religious order school.[6]

Table 3.2

Vocational Status of Those Serving as Rectors/Presidents

	Diocesan Priests		Religious Priests	
	Number	*Percent*	*Number*	*Percent*
2015	25	64.1	14	35.9
1999	22	52.4	20	47.6
1989	22	44.9	27	55.1

The academic credentials of the leaders of theologates are similar to those in the past, with nearly three-fourths holding doctoral degrees (74.4 percent in 1989, 71.4 percent in 1999, and 71.8 percent in 2015). The remaining leaders hold STL or master-level degrees. In recent years, seminary administrators and faculty were urged to obtain pontifical degrees if they did not already hold them. Among rectors/presidents, the proportion has grown modestly from 51.2 in 1989, to 57.1 in 1999, to 61.5 percent in 2015.

The fields of study of rectors/presidents changed significantly from 1989 to 2015 in several areas. For each time period the areas of study of a few leaders are unknown.

- Degrees in pastoral theology dropped from twelve in 1989 to seven in 1999 to only one in 2015.

---

religious institutes. A further variation is Oblate School of Theology, a free-standing theologate whose CEO is called "president" and included in this discussion; the rector of the associated house of formation for diocesan seminarians, Assumption Seminary, is not included here. Finally, Sacred Heart Seminary and School of Theology offers a complete program on its own; the seminarians from the Archdiocese of Milwaukee take all aspects of formation except academic at Saint Francis de Sales Seminary.

[6] A diocesan priest began his term as president of Aquinas Institute in 2014, the first person who is not a Dominican friar to serve in that capacity in its eighty-eight-year history.

- Those with education and psychology degrees dropped from five in 1989 and 1999 to none in 2015.

- Degrees in canon law increased from none in the first two periods to seven in 2015. One rector, new in 2015, holds a civil law degree. All those with canon law degrees lead diocesan seminaries.

- Degrees in theology (systematic, moral, or other) remained steady at sixteen.

- Those with degrees in Scripture, philosophy, and liturgy remained steady at four each.

Another notable change is the length of service and the turnover in leadership of rectors/presidents in recent years. In the 1980s the average time in office was 6.4 years; since the 2000s, terms ended after 4.8 years. At the beginning of the 2014–15 academic year, 67.5 percent had served less than 5 years as CEOs. As each 10-year period commenced, beginning in 2004, the proportion with 5 years or less experience was 65 percent, decreasing to 46 percent in 1994 and to 33 percent in 1984. Three new CEOs were appointed in 2015, which brings the proportion to 75 percent. The rapid and widespread turnover can have a negative effect on an individual seminary, but of broader consequence is the loss of the wisdom of experienced leaders. The perception of their role and the way it is exercised provide a window into how rectors/presidents function. The differences detailed below show that their perceptions may be based on having more or less experience, serving in different types of seminaries, and coming from older or younger age groups.

Viewpoints and outlooks. Several studies have analyzed the role of rectors/presidents in recent years. They call attention to the responsibility these leaders have for setting tone, establishing priorities, and providing structures for the support of all members of the theologate community. Current rectors/presidents concur with these requirements. The survey for this book probed the role further by seeking the views of rectors/presidents about what gifts and skills they thought were most important, the strengths they brought, and their most significant accomplishments. Analysis of their responses included three categories: the type of seminary they were leading—diocesan-sponsored, religious order-sponsored for diocesan seminarians, and those operated by and for religious orders; the number of years of service—those with less than 5 years and those with 5 years or more; and the ages of the respondents—under 55 and 55 or older.

As CEOs reflected on important *gifts and skills* that helped them lead, the seventy or so comments related to three main areas: the mission of the seminary, their own backgrounds, and the virtues and qualities they thought most important in fulfilling their role. Concerning *the mission*, two distinct views were evident: first, having a clear vision about the mission, understanding it, and promoting it in a way that demonstrated a clear pathway to the future; and second, expressed in more immediate terms, being able to pastor the community with love for seminarians and the priesthood, as well as others being formed for ministry. The first focused on a broad leadership role that was more externally oriented than the second, which was more internally focused on pastoral care for seminarians and other students. The responses below exemplify the two positions:

> [A rector should be] one who collaborates with others in defining, promoting, and living the Vatican II mission of the institution. [He] is an academic leader, assists in having the institution be student-centered, is the public face to the larger culture and assists in advancement opportunities. With the dean, [he] provides faculty development opportunities while also working with staff in a diversified environment. [He] is in a shared governance relationship with the board of trustees and ecclesial/religious endorsers [and] works closely with others for fiscal management of the institution while looking to grow enrollment.

> I believe a good rector must be good with people and patient with others' shortcomings. The office of rector is primarily one of teaching, and the best teacher is example. For many seminarians, the first encounter they will have with a church authority figure is the rector. Thus, the rector must always keep in mind that how he acts and responds to issues of the day may very well set the pattern that seminarians may follow. The rector should be a good pastor and teacher so that seminarians can model their behavior on his. This requires a great deal of humility on the part of the rector. He should be able to apologize when necessary, even in public if he makes a mistake, and should be careful of doing anything that can be seen as arrogant and self-serving.

Leaders of schools associated with religious orders and those who had served as CEOs for 5 years or more emphasized the broader conception of the mission. Diocesan rectors and those who had served less than 5 years identified more closely with the pastoral role. Age was not a determining factor in that the leadership focus and the pastoral focus were equally supported by those over 55 and those 55 and under.

Relative to their *ministerial or professional backgrounds*, about half the respondents mentioned previous positions they considered important in exercising their current role as CEOs. Most common was pastoral ministry in a parish, followed by administration and teaching, especially helpful if it was located in a seminary. Those who were new to their positions were more likely to make reference to their backgrounds, especially diocesan rectors. More than half the comments concerned the *virtues and qualities* they thought most important in fulfilling their role. The virtues named as essential by these leaders correspond well to the nature of their positions regardless of the type of school, age, or length of service. Being prudent and patient topped the list, followed closely by having integrity and being authentic, honest, and charitable. The necessity of being rooted in prayer was expressed in many ways. Mention of desirable qualities revealed the wide range of approaches employed by CEOs, including styles of managing, ways of relating to authority, and personal traits. They considered engaging in effective communication and using collaboration as a regular method of working together as crucial. Several comments about relationship with the church were identified as necessary: embracing the teaching of the church, being loyal to the magisterium, and having a great love for the priesthood. Respondents named other personal traits to be of particular value, such as being responsible and dependable, being flexible and imaginative, and having a sense of humor.

CEOs were asked to identify the *strengths* they bring to their ministry. Many of the responses matched or complemented their previous observations about the gifts and skills they thought were important. Three categories stood out: their background experiences, leadership and organizational skills, and love for the church and priesthood. Most of them recognized strengths in more than one area, as expressed in these comments.

- "I have served in a wide variety of ministries and have brought that background. I have a deep love of the priesthood and strong pastoral bent. I have learned to consult and am able to make hard decisions as needed. I can inspire others."
- "[I have had] extensive education and formation background in multiple ministry experiences; significant training in the area of human formation; decent administration and communication skills."
- "[I bring a] love of the church universal and local, including all our ministerial candidates; lots of experience in parish life and in the area of theology—teaching and research and publishing."

- "[I have the] capacity to build consensus and support the faculty and staff, ability to work with the Board and [give] attention to the constituencies of the school."

Their *backgrounds* in ministry and in other areas of work before becoming seminary CEOs ranged from pastoral and parish ministry to teaching and administration in a variety of settings. As might be expected, diocesan rectors were more likely to identify their parish ministries and work in diocesan offices. Religious order CEOs most frequently listed educational ministries, especially in theologates. Older CEOs pinpointed previous seminary experiences and younger ones often mentioned their extensive education and pastoral ministry.

A second set of strengths was related to *leadership and organizational skills*. Most often respondents identified a style of leadership that was shared, with commitment to consensus-building, consultation, collaboration, and delegation. Closely related was the ability to be relational with a wide range of constituents from board members and donors, to faculty, staff, and students. Most effective was an approach to management that was direct, sincere, and fair, as well as creative, enthusiastic, and joyful. The third category of leadership strengths was somewhat less tangible but important to the ministry: love of the church, of priesthood, and of seminarians. These CEOs described their commitment to the mission and vision of their seminary, that is, to formation work and to the future ministry of seminarians. Their strengths corresponded closely to the ways leaders understood their roles and responsibilities as CEOs.

CEOs were asked to identify their two most *significant accomplishments*. Their comments were divided between achievements concerning internal operations (55 percent) and those dealing with external relationships and activities (45 percent).

Internal achievements related to the overall vision of formation as indicated by the great attention given to the review, revision, renewal, and development of programs in all areas. The resulting changes encompassed integration of all four formation pillars or areas, especially important for those preparing diocesan candidates in a freestanding seminary. Religious order CEOs were more likely to focus on reorganizing and revitalizing academic degrees and establishing new degrees that were consistent with the principles of servant leadership for seminarians and lay students. Distributed proportionately among all types of schools were other internal accomplishments such as dealing with spiritual renewal for the whole community made possible by hiring well-qualified faculty and staff and providing for faculty development. Several rectors spoke of their accomplishments in terms of restoring and/or building community and encouraging a greater sense of involvement among faculty with the goal of awakening an awareness of the importance of organizational culture as formative. This effort entailed developing consensus among faculty and formation team members on what would be the nature of the renewed vision for formation. One rector expressed this accomplishment as "expanding the collaboration between the faculty of all four pillars—particularly between intellectual formation faculty and the other pillars." Others noted the following:

- "I have worked particularly closely with several seminarians who have struggled greatly and have been able to both challenge and support them and help them move forward. We also have been able to continue recruiting future priest-faculty and arrange for their further studies."

- "Creating a sense of urgency that the Seminary move forward with an agenda for change. Rector's conferences on a regular and consistent basis on topics of priestly identity, celibacy, and being men of integrity and holiness."

- "Sharing what I have learned in forty-six years of priesthood with the seminarians in rector's conferences and personal conversations and with all students in the classroom."

External achievements were marked by four interrelated themes: outreach to become better known, to increase enrollment, to gain financial support, and to establish new relationships. Several rectors/presidents identified specific external successes in their ministry outside the institution:

- "Having established a committee to increase our profile and our outreach on the internet; having expanded our donor base."

- "Increasing the enrollment of the seminary three-fold without compromising the quality of educational and human standards."

- "I am in the process of restructuring our institutional advancement office within the scope of a newly formed archdiocesan office and redoing our antiquated website."

- "Assisting the graduate school into the first iteration of a strategic plan and built a relationship with the USCCB by planning/hosting a first-ever conference for bishops."

Outreach to members of the boards of trustees was considered especially beneficial in that it led to personal connections with a variety of other constituencies. While these contacts are valuable for fundraising and increasing enrollment, they also provide an opportunity to serve others. A diocesan rector said that he found it useful to collaborate with a wide range of people in defining, promoting, and living the Vatican II mission of the institution as well as providing spiritual enrichment to them.

Summary and analysis. The shape of the mission and vision of a theologate is determined more by the CEO than any other person involved with the organization. In analyzing the comments from the survey of these leaders, at least three factors differentiate them, namely, the length of time of service in the role, their fields of study, and the focus of the mission and vision, that is, their understanding of what their institution should be and do.

- One fact stands out above all others: the nearly 75 percent turnover among those leading diocesan and religious order theologates. Individual schools are affected by a lack of continuity, but most concerning is the loss of a sense of the evolution and progression of these institutions as a body, a loss of the history of seminary education. At the same time, other key leaders of supporting organizations have changed and, in the case of the NCEA Seminary Department, have been disbanded. Other structures that might bring CEOs together are being explored, but it will take time before they can establish and become proficient in developing leadership skills and institutional structures.

- Another significant change is in the fields of study of the CEOs. Pastoral theology degrees dropped from twelve in 1989 to only one at present; seven now hold canon law degrees and one a civil law degree, a change from none in 1989 and 1999. In recent years, a high percentage of diocesan priests in advanced studies have pursued canon law degrees, so it is not surprising that they are now serving as diocesan rectors/presidents. Unknown are the effects of this shift in nearly thirty percent of diocesan seminaries being headed by them.

- The distinct interpretations of the role of rector/president is also notable. A nearly even split occurs between those who understand the position as more external (convener/leader) and more internal (pastor/leader). The gifts and skills needed for each vary somewhat, but more distinctive is the background they bring to the position. Those who focus on the larger external situation and the broader constituency of the theologate often come from a background that encompasses teaching, administration, and some pastoral ministry. Those who focus on the internal communal dimensions, with special concern for preparation of seminarians as future priests, tend to have been pastors or associates before their studies and then moved into seminary leadership.

2. Other Senior Administrators

As mentioned above, the number and variety of administrative positions have grown tremendously in recent years. At the same time, traditional positions comprising top-level administration have remained in place—academic deans, vice rectors, and vice presidents. At least some of the growth can be attributed to an increase in the diversity of students. Enrollment, for example, now includes many more international seminarians and lay students in most schools. New and expanded activities such as human formation, lay degree programs, and introduction of STB degrees requiring relationships with Roman institutions account for other increases. Beyond programmatic changes, many staff have been added for recruitment and development activities. Most expansion has occurred at the level of director and is part of existing areas and departments.

Academic deans. Every theologate has a designated administrator responsible for academic leadership. "Dean" is the most common title for this position; twenty of the thirty-nine schools use "academic dean." Five university-related schools use simply "dean," where the dean is also the CEO of the theologate; in one other university-related school, the CEO has two titles—rector and dean. In some freestanding seminaries, academic leadership is provided by the dean of academic formation or dean of studies. Other names for the position vary considerably; in six schools vice president is part of the title and in two schools the vice rector is the dean. Three schools use "director" as part of the title for the academic leader. The titles are significant in that they designate the level and extent of responsibility. In most diocesan schools they are one of the three major administrators, along with rectors/presidents and vice-rectors, who exercise broad leadership for the entire school as well as oversight of the academic area, and sometimes they teach as well. In religious order schools they are often the chief administrator.

The broader role of academic deans has affected changes in highest degrees, rank, and vocational status. During the last twenty-five years, the proportion of those with doctorates grew to 95 percent from 77 percent, and considerably more now are given rank and they more often hold the rank of professor (see appendix 3-A and appendix 3-B). In the 1980s almost all academic deans were priests; half were diocesan and 43 percent were men religious. At present the role is filled equally by diocesan priests, religious priests, and laymen at 30.8 percent each. Few women have occupied the position through the years, with three (7.5 percent) at present (see appendix 3-C). The academic fields of deans have remained fairly steady, with most holding degrees in systematic theology (see appendix 3-D).

Given the changes in the dean's role, the academic area now involves numerous administrative staff who usually report to them. Two of these positions carry faculty status, namely, the library director and the director of pastoral formation or field education, which are considered later in this chapter under faculty. All diocesan theologates employ a director of library services (with one exception)[7] and many library staff. Only three of the nine theologates for religious have a separate theological library since the others make use of the library at the university with which they are affiliated.[8] Similarly, most theologates have a registrar, though that person often has other duties such as director of admissions or of student services. Some theologates associated with universities have their own registrar, but others use the services of the university. More common than ever before are multiple directors of degree programs and of areas such as second language and cultural studies, especially for Hispanics. The directors of music and liturgy are often the same person in diocesan seminaries,[9] but about a dozen of them have separated the functions into two distinct positions. About 90 percent of program directors are related to the academic area.

---

[7] The Catholic University of America provides library services for seminarians who live at Theological College, which does not have a separate library.

[8] The three are Dominican House of Studies, Washington, DC; Boston College School of Theology and Ministry, Chestnut Hill, MA; and Catholic Theological Union, Chicago, IL. The circumstances are similar in that the first two are or were independent institutions, with their own extensive theological libraries. CTU has always been an independent institution with its own library.

[9] Since religious order seminarians live in their own formation houses, faculty members oversee school liturgies, which are less frequently offered at the school.

Vice rectors, vice presidents, and formation department leaders. Of the twenty-nine diocesan seminaries, twenty-three have a priest serving as vice rector, fourteen of whom hold another position, most commonly in a specific area of formation. Three schools have more than one vice rector. The role of vice rectors varies, but the majority are responsible for human formation or formation in general. They usually join the rector on a council or administrative team. Of the six diocesan schools that do not have a vice rector, most of them collaborate with a seminary where their students reside and receive human and spiritual formation. Vice rectors are part of the rectors' staff and those under their supervision are formation directors. None of the religious order schools have a vice rector.

Vice presidents are named in sixteen theologates, including both diocesan and religious. Generally their designated responsibilities are in academics, administration, or finances. Two schools have multiple vice presidents, one with four and the other with six. The size of the school often dictates the number of separate administrative positions. In fourteen diocesan seminaries the dean of students (or a similar title) is part of the CEO's administrative team. Religious order theologates often employ directors of students and/or student services for lay students, but usually they do not serve on the council. Since most theologates are relatively small, some combine the positions related to institutional advancement/ development and finance, but fifteen of the thirty-nine use the services of both officers. The size of staffs working in institutional advancement/ development are often larger because they deal with marketing, communications, and sometimes with admissions (which alternately may be part of the academic dean's office). When business and finance directors are not associated with development, they sometimes serve as facilities managers, but in half the theologates, the position of director of facilities or plant manager stands on its own.

Every theologate employs administrative leaders for all or some of the four elements of formation—human, spiritual, academic, pastoral. As described above, the position of academic dean is firmly established and most have employed a director of field education for a long time. Still evolving is the structure and leadership of human and spiritual formation. Prior to the introduction of the term "human formation" by Pope John Paul II in *Pastores Dabo Vobis* in 1992, the terms used in diocesan seminaries were "personal and spiritual formation," almost always led by the director of spiritual formation. For the past ten years or so, many leaders have changed the organization of human and spiritual formation for seminarians, often redefining roles and expanding positions. Common names and structures have not yet been established, but twenty diocesan schools have a designated leader: fourteen have a director or dean of human formation and eleven of them also have a director of spiritual formation; seven have a director or dean of formation, including one school that has both a dean and a director. The others have only a director of spiritual formation or have an associated residence that provides formation for students.[10] Fewer than ten theologates employ a resident psychologist, but psychological services are available to virtually all diocesan seminarians. Most aspects of human and spiritual formation take place in religious order communities where related services are provided.

Summary and analysis. Administrative roles and structures have changed considerably during the past thirty years as theologates have grown in complexity and diversity though usually not in size. The newly defined positions are related to program expansion, a more diverse student population, and additional formation positions. When taking into account the positions identified above, the number of administrators varies according to the programs and students; the average per school is about fifteen administrators, and the range is from ten to just over thirty. Not represented are the many staff positions at the level of administrative assistants, technology experts, and secretaries. The financial layout for salaries has grown faster than inflation and, for some schools, the expense has become a serious concern for future viability.

C. Faculty

Introduction

Theologate faculties, which constitute the third component of leadership, exercise substantial direct influence on students and thus on shaping future church ministry. Their roles are multiple, including teaching and formation advising, as well as research, writing, and speaking. To understand clearly the nature of their impact, it is important to know how their vocational status, credentials, and sources of degrees have changed since the 1980s.[11] In surveys, personal interviews, and at annual gatherings of

---

[10] See chapter 5 for details on the content of human and spiritual formation.

[11] This background information has been amassed from catalogs from the early 1980s to the present.

faculty and administrators, faculty members expressed their views and attitudes on topics such as hiring, retention, and salaries, as well as on formation and teaching experiences. Some of this data is reported here and some in the sections dealing with the particular topic of the inquiries. The data is inclusive of all those listed as full-time faculty by each school, and, even if they are not on the faculty list, all CEOs, pastoral/field education directors, and librarians, who usually are considered faculty by accrediting agencies.

Faculty Composition and Roles

The numbers and composition of faculty changed considerably over the past thirty years, corresponding to church directives[12] and changes in availability of priests to serve in theologates. At the same time, their roles incorporated new responsibilities related to the content and understanding of formation and in dealing with more international and non-Anglo students. In 1985, faculty numbered 898; by 1995 that number had decreased by 157 to 741. It rose slightly to 783 by 2005, and it reached 871 by 2015 even as the number of theologates continued to drop from 52 in 1985 to 39 in 2015. The average size of faculties increased only slightly from 17.3 in 1985 to 17.6 in 1995 and to 17.8 in 2005, but, because of fewer schools, the average size grew much more by 2015 to 22.3.

From 1985 to 1995, the number of seminarians declined sharply from 4,150 to 3,280, and then rose to 3,650 by 2015; lay student numbers remained steady at about 3,000. With 500 fewer seminarians and 13 fewer

[12] For example, in the 2005 *PPF* 346–48, the directives about faculty were explicit in terms of required backgrounds, credentials, and vocational status. Number 346 addresses the preferred source of degrees: "The professors should have advanced, preferably terminal, degrees in their teaching areas. Professors in the sacred sciences, as well as philosophy, should possess a doctorate or licentiate from a university or institution recognized by the Holy See. Priest faculty members should have appropriate experience in pastoral ministry." (On the same topic, see also the report on the Apostolic Visitation of American seminaries, December 15, 2008.) Number 347 deals with vocational status: "As a general rule, professors for significant portions of the course of studies in the major theological disciplines ought to be priests" (according to *Ratio Fundamentalis* 33). Number 348 allows for other qualified faculty to serve in theologates: "Priests who are responsible for the human, spiritual, intellectual, and pastoral dimensions of priestly formation can be assisted by outstanding laypersons and/or non-ordained religious, all of whom have a particular expertise that can contribute to priestly formation" (see *PDV* 66).

theologates than thirty years ago, the faculty census is almost the same and the student-faculty ratio is similar. Taking into account the total student body (seminarians and lay students), the student/faculty ratios were 8 to 1 in 1985, 8.5 to 1 in 1995, 8.1 to 1 in 2005, and 7.6 to 1 in 2015. In addition, the number of adjunct faculty increased greatly through the years, resulting in an even lower student-faculty ratio. The diversity of roles for faculty and the expansion of programs account for much of the increase.

Student and faculty size vary considerably from school to school, as do the functions of faculty.[13] In religious order theologates, few faculty serve as formation advisers to seminarians since that work is performed in religious communities, but many advise lay students. Lay students are distributed unequally among schools, ranging from none to over a hundred, thus affecting advisory duties. Other variations, such as publication expectations and weekend parish assignments, also contribute to uneven workloads. In many cases, diocesan priests are listed as full-time faculty, but have obligations elsewhere, including diocesan offices, parishes, and chaplaincies at other institutions. In 1985, only about 10 percent of faculties had significant responsibilities beyond teaching and research. That figure rose to 30 percent in 1995 and is now almost 50 percent. As a result, the role faculty plays in the formation of students and in the development and staffing of programs diverges considerably from earlier years.

Vocational Status

Besides the number of faculty, another conspicuous shift since the 1980s is their vocational status, with almost every group differing in size and influence. Most notable is the decrease in the proportion of priests from 76 percent in 1985 to 56 percent in 2015 (see table 3.3). However, the loss is almost entirely of men religious, whose numbers are down by nearly 200 compared to a decline of just 20 among diocesan priests. The reason for the change has historical roots. When numerous religious order theologates closed in the late 1960s, many of the faculty migrated to diocesan seminaries. By now most of them have reached retirement age, so only a few men religious are still teaching at these schools. For the most part, lay faculty have replaced them. Almost all of the 30.5 percent of current

---

[13] In some of the fifteen theologates with university ties, faculty teach many other students who are not preparing for ministry, but since they also teach seminarians and lay ministry students, they are counted here.

Table 3.3

Vocational Status of Faculty by Year

	1985	1995	2005	2015
Diocesan priests	32.5%	33.2%	28.1%	30.5%
Men religious	43.7	32.8	28.7	25.5
ALL PRIESTS	**76.2**	**66.0**	**56.8**	**56.0**
Laymen	9.8	14.6	22.0	25.3
ALL MEN	**86.0**	**80.6**	**78.8**	**81.3**
Laywomen	3.7	6.6	12.3	13.8
Women religious	10.4	12.8	8.9	4.9
ALL WOMEN	**14.1**	**19.4**	**21.2**	**18.7**

faculty who are diocesan priests serve in seminaries operated by dioceses; most of the 25.5 percent who are men religious staff their own seminaries and eight diocesan seminaries operated by a religious order. The number of laymen on faculty increased more than any other vocational group, from 88 (9.8 percent) in 1985 to 220 (25.3 percent) in 2015. Laywomen, who represent a much smaller percentage of faculty members, also increased in number. In 1985, there were only 33 laywomen nationally serving on theologate faculties (3.7 percent), and now there are 120 (13.8 percent). The number of women religious faculty members substantially declined from 93 (10.4 percent) in 1985 to 43 (4.9 percent) in 2015, reflecting the steady decrease in the total number of sisters. A closer look at the patterns related to the role of women in theologates follows later.

The focal points of change in vocational status are as follows:

- The proportion of priests, almost entirely men religious, has dropped by over 20 percent, with the sharpest decline between 1985 and 1995; this decline, though not as dramatic, has continued to the present.

- The overall proportion of men, ordained and lay, declined by almost 5 percent, but has remained stable for twenty years; the proportion of laymen increased gradually by 15 percent since 1985.

- The proportion of women stayed steady at nearly 20 percent for twenty years; since 1985, the proportion of laywomen has increased by 10 percent and the proportion of women religious has declined by 5 percent.

Credentials

Church leaders have supported a high level of academic expertise for those who serve as theologate faculty. Each of the five editions of the *PPF* urge diocesan bishops and religious ordinaries "to provide excellent and competent faculty" and to be "generous in encouraging priests to prepare for seminary work or in releasing their priests for this ministry, even if the seminary is not their own" (*PPF* V 347). In 1985, two-thirds of theologate faculty members held doctoral degrees; in 2015 three-fourths had doctorates (see table 3.4). The somewhat lower increase among diocesan priests can be attributed to the fact that many of them serve in formation roles that usually do not require a doctoral degree; also, because of the need to hire many of them in a short time to meet new formation and advising duties, they were not given time to earn an advanced degree. The proportion of laywomen with doctorates, though now higher than in earlier years, is at only 68.3 percent, in part because a higher proportion of them teach in pastoral areas. The 2005 *PPF* prescribed that significant portions of the courses in the major theological disciplines be taught by priests.

Table 3.4

Faculty Degrees by Vocational Status and Years

	Diocesan Priests	Men Religious	Women Religious	Laymen	Laywomen	Total
Doctoral Degrees						
1985	59.6	77.6	53.8	67.0	54.5	67.4
1995	63.4	84.8	66.3	86.1	71.4	74.6
2005	65.0	87.6	72.9	83.7	56.3	75.2
2015	61.6	85.2	80.5	86.2	68.3	75.6
Other Degrees						
1985	40.4	22.4	46.2	33.0	45.5	32.6
1995	36.6	15.2	33.7	13.9	28.6	25.4
2005	35.0	12.4	27.1	16.3	43.7	24.8
2015	38.4	14.8	19.5	13.8	31.7	24.4

Sources of Degrees

Over 70 percent of the highest degrees held by faculty were granted by numerous universities throughout the United States, both Catholic and non-Catholic institutions. Most of the remaining faculty were awarded degrees from European schools, largely from Roman pontifical universities (see table 3.5). The proportion of those degrees gradually decreased between the mid-1980s and 2015 by about 7 percent, from 25.7 to 18.9 percent. During the same period, the decrease in pontifical degrees was 11 percent. Although *PPF* V 346 states that professors in certain fields should have earned a degree from a university or institution recognized by the Holy See, that is, a pontifical institution, the proportion of faculty holding those desired degrees has declined significantly. During the same period, American Catholic universities increased by 4 percent and non-Catholic American universities by 7.7 percent.

Table 3.5

Sources of Highest Academic Degrees of Faculty by Year

Years[14]	1985		1995		2005		2015	
Schools	#	%	#	%	#	%	#	%
Roman Pontifical Schools	190	25.7	208	23.2	170	21.7	153	18.9
University of Louvain	38	5.1	23	2.5	15	1.9	15	1.9
Other European Universities	72	9.7	62	6.9	50	6.4	72	8.9[15]
Catholic University of America	86	11.6	111	12.4	76	9.7	84	10.4
American Catholic Universities	222	30.0	303	33.7	246	31.4	276	34.2[16]

continued next page

[14] Years are approximate since most catalogs were issued every two or three years until recently, when schools began publishing them online.

[15] Includes degrees from European universities (64), other pontifical universities (4), and other non-European universities (Israel 2, Mexico 1, and Australia 1), for a total of 72.

[16] Includes degrees from American Catholic universities (166), Canadian universities (18), and American theologates (92) for a total of 276.

Table 3.5

Sources of Highest Academic Degrees of Faculty by Year (continued)

Years	1985		1995		2005		2015	
Schools	#	%	#	%	#	%	#	%
Non-Catholic American Universities	133	18.0	191	21.3	227	28.9	208	25.7
TOTAL	741	100.1	898	100.0	784	100.0[17]	808	100.0[18]
					(of 836 total)		(of 871 total)	

Noteworthy findings concerning credentials and sources of degrees are as follows:

- The proportion of faculty holding doctoral degrees is 75.6 percent, an increase of 8 percent since 1985.

- Responsibility for spiritual direction and increased formation advising by diocesan priests has kept the proportion of doctorates at a relatively low level.

- The sources of degrees have shifted gradually from European to American universities.

- The proportion having earned their highest degree from a pontifical university has dropped by 11 percent, from 42.4 percent to 31.4 percent, though many of the others have a licentiate from a pontifical university.

Hiring, Salaries, and Retention

The numbers of faculty and their roles have changed substantially in recent years, necessitating frequent faculty searches. The rectors' survey provided significant information about the most desirable characteristics in the search for faculty. The two qualities considered crucial or very important were the ability to integrate areas of formation (97 percent) and having

---

[17] In 2005, the total faculty was 836, with 784 faculty degree sources identified, 52 missing.

[18] In 2015, the total faculty was 871, with 808 faculty degree sources identified, 63 missing.

a compatible theological/ecclesial perspective (94 percent). For diocesan faculties, the next highest priority was having a pastoral background (79 percent) and for religious the source of the academic degrees mattered (78 percent). Surprisingly, less than half (47 percent) of all respondents chose ethnic diversity as crucial. Choices varied by age of respondents and their years of service; older, more experienced leaders were more likely to focus on the importance of pastoral experience, while the younger, less experienced chose ability to integrate areas of formation. Two other characteristics frequently identified as desirable were being collaborative and understanding the mission of the school.

Those who ultimately will be hired is determined in large part by the pool of candidates. With fewer men religious available, the number of laymen has increased significantly since 2000, and with fewer women religious available, the number of laywomen also has grown. The addition of more than one hundred laymen and about seventy laywomen to theologate faculties has had further impact: their backgrounds usually focus on academic preparation, but not on other aspects of formation; familiarity with the particular diocese or religious order is often not as extensive as that of priests and religious; and salary and benefit requirements are more substantial. As a consequence, theologates need to provide more thorough orientation and ongoing education and formation for these specialized positions and more resources are needed to support lay faculty. Theologates have not responded fully to these new circumstances with programs and resources, and so the full potential of these new faculty members has not yet been realized.

Another consideration in hiring concerns the presence of women as faculty members. The survey asked if the more limited roles available for women since the 2005 *PPF* were of concern, and if so, in what ways it was a concern. In response, 39 percent said the restriction was not a concern and 61 percent said it was. Two opinions about women faculty prevailed. On one side, the respondents who seek to hire more women said they have ascertained that it is more difficult to recruit qualified women, given the roles that are discouraged (such as teaching in the major theological disciplines or directing field education programs) or actually excluded (such as engaging in formation advising or giving spiritual direction). These respondents noted that this situation is a loss to the church since seminarians will be in professional ministerial relationships with women more often than with men and would benefit from interacting with women faculty. They also appreciated the perspective women can bring to the entire formation process. Several referred to Scripture as a basis for their views; one person stated, "From biblical times, women have had a strong and influential role in organizing, conducting, and supporting a host of ministries in the Church."

On the other side, the restrictions in hiring women were seen as advantageous by some for these reasons: the critical role of accompanying seminarians requires multiple levels of knowledge about them so that they can be mentored into spiritual fatherhood and spousal identities as future priests; some faculty and bishops have concern about the ability of women to relate pastorally; and church documents want only priests to fulfill certain roles, although some teaching and administrative duties can be fulfilled by women. Responses were not differentiated by the age of CEOs or the years of service, though some variation was evident in the type of school.

The need for new hires is precipitated by a rather low long-term retention rate and normal retirement among faculty, with the pace of change increasing especially in the past fifteen years. From 1988 to about 2000, 36 percent of faculty were retained, 30 percent for diocesan and 50 percent for religious order theologates. During the second time period from about 2000 to 2014, retention overall was 25 percent—21 percent for diocesan and 33 percent for religious. The rates at individual schools varied tremendously, from 5 percent to 67 percent retention in the first period and 5 percent to 44 percent in the second period. Considering faculty longevity over time, less than 6 percent of those who were teaching in 1988, only fifty-one, are still teaching today. The vast majority, thirty-one of those who continue, are men religious. Of the remaining twenty, eight are laymen, six diocesan priests, five laywomen, and one woman religious. Men religious who teach in seminaries often make it their lifelong vocation, but diocesan priests who have served in the past are often appointed to diocesan positions, including a large number as bishops or as pastors. The proportionately smaller number of faculty in other categories sometimes move to teaching in Catholic colleges and universities and many have retired. On the whole, theologate faculty are comprised almost totally of a new generation whose experiences of church and society are vastly different from the generation that preceded them. Faculty satisfaction and concerns will be treated in later chapters dealing with students and programs.

Faculty Serving as Directors of Pastoral Formation and Field Education

In many respects, pastoral formation is the responsibility of all faculty, including those who administer the field education program, those who teach pastoral courses, and those who moderate theological reflection with groups of students. Those on the faculty responsible for field education or, as it is commonly called, supervised ministry have unique and essential duties, including judicious oversight and evaluation of students in the settings where they engage in ministry. Besides seminary personnel, parish field supervisors, parish committees and staff engage in this aspect of formation. Others outside of parish settings, such as in hospitals, prisons, and schools, also contribute to onsite supervision.

The title associated with the position of director is divided between field education (12) and pastoral formation (25) with three additional schools using both designations. Compared to fifteen years ago, the title change pattern is reversed as more theologates are now using pastoral formation to name the directors and those who assist them. The vocational status of the directors also shifted through the years (see table 3.6), with a higher proportion of priests in 2015.

Table 3.6

Vocational Status of Directors of Pastoral Formation/Field Education

	1989		1999		2015	
	Number/Percent		*Number/Percent*		*Number/Percent*	
Diocesan Priests	16	33.3	14	33.3	19	47.5
Men Religious	11	22.9	5	11.9	6	15.0
Women Religious	16	33.3	14	33.3	4	10.0
Laywomen	3	6.3	6	14.3	10	25.0
Laymen	1	2.1	1	2.4	-	-
Other	1*	2.1	2*	4.8	1**	2.5
TOTAL	48		42		40***	
*Protestant Ministers **Deacon ***One school has codirectors						

Currently, 65 percent are ordained (one director is a deacon). This represents about 10 percent more than in 1989, and nearly 20 percent more than in 1999. The opposite trend is found in the proportion of women religious who serve in this role, down from 33 percent in 1989 and 1999 to 10 percent in 2015.[19]

The proportion of directors who are granted formal academic rank is 50 percent, only a slight increase from 47.6 percent in 1999, but 12.5 percent more than the 37.5 percent in 1989. Adjuncts and some formation faculty are among those who are not ranked. The 50 percent currently ranked is the same proportion as of those who hold terminal degrees, up by 8 percent from 1989 and by nearly 17 percent from 1999 (see table 3.7). By these measures, the overall status of directors has improved somewhat since the 1980s.

Table 3.7

Terminal Degree of Directors of Pastoral Formation/Field Education

Degree	1989 Number/Percent		1999 Number/Percent		2015 Number/Percent	
PhD	10		7		9	
STD	2	41.9%	4	33.3%	5	50.0%
DMin	6		3		5	
STL	0		0		2	
MDiv	8		9		6	
MA	16	58.1%	18	66.7%	10	50.0%
BA/BS	1		1		0	
STB	0		0		1	
TOTAL	43		42		38	

[19] The drastic reduction in the number of women religious is no doubt due in part to the decrease in women religious in general and is also related to the directive in *PPF* V 340, which states: "If the director of pastoral formation is more than an organizer of field education experiences, then this position should be filled by a priest." Since directors have a much broader role, as described in chapter 6 on academic and pastoral formation programs, the restriction has been followed in many theologates, except that in religious order schools, seven of ten directors are laywomen, and in diocesan schools three women religious and four laywomen still hold the director's position.

The role of supervised ministry will be elaborated further in chapter 6, which deals with academic and pastoral formation programs.

Summary and Analysis

Faculty contribute substantially to all aspects of theologate organization and operations; in particular they have an expansive impact on the lives of students as teachers and advisers. Those whose role is teaching need expertise not only in their discipline, but also in knowing how to apply their discipline to pastoral ministry. Those whose role is formation advising need to understand how to help seminarians develop the human and spiritual qualities necessary for priestly life and ministry. Most priests have considerable responsibilities in both areas and all faculty should recognize the importance of all dimensions of formation. Therefore, the principal considerations in hiring and retaining faculty include balancing the composition of faculty by vocational status, gender, and backgrounds so that they can serve both seminarians and lay students; orienting and educating new faculty for the unique role of preparing students in all areas of formation and for the particular dioceses and church ministries where they will minister; providing adequate resources to fairly compensate the growing number of lay faculty; and making available ongoing education and insisting that all faculty take advantage of opportunities that are offered.

PART III

Students Preparing for Ministry
Enrollment and Programs

Chapter 4

Seminarians and Lay Students

Introduction

The capability of the church in the United States to meet the spiritual needs of the growing and changing Catholic population depends on the qualities and numbers of men and women preparing for ministry. Discussions about seminaries often turn to the question, "What are the seminarians like?" The answer is complex because of the great diversity among them, both within a particular school and in the entire seminary system as a whole. Lay ministry students are equally diverse, but data about them is not as complete since they have a shorter history of enrollment in theologates and they are more likely to be enrolled in programs at other institutions. Nonetheless, the church needs an adequate number of both groups of students for effective ministry in the future.

This chapter analyzes student data from the thirty-nine seminaries and schools of theology that are part of this study and includes trends in numbers and other measurable characteristics. Almost all of the men who will be future priests in the United States are enrolled in these schools.[1] This is true as well for a significant proportion of lay women and men studying for degrees for service in parishes, dioceses, and other Catholic institutions. For many years CARA has collected information about where

[1] In most cases, seminarians coming from other countries attend a diocesan or religious order theologate in the United States. Priests coming from all over the world in gradually increasing numbers usually have attended seminaries and were ordained in their own countries.

75

students for ordained and lay ministry were enrolled, including racial/ethnic backgrounds, countries of origin, and ages. Also considered here is data from the rectors' survey concerning seminarians and the formational and special needs of international students. In addition, comments by rectors/presidents whose schools enroll lay students reflect on the value of their presence and their relationships with seminarians. The chapter concludes with a discussion of the implications about how well those preparing for ministry might meet the requirements of an increasingly diverse Catholic population.

Since 1967–68 CARA has collected extensive data about seminarians and since 1994–95 about lay students. For nearly fifty years the accumulated data on seminarians and for twenty years on lay ministry students have provided valuable information to dioceses and institutions as they plan to address the pastoral and spiritual needs of a growing number of Catholics in the United States. The following descriptions give an indication of the numbers and characteristics of each group.[2]

A. Seminarians

Numbers. Wide variation in the number of seminarians enrolled from year to year in theologates is evident ever since data was first collected. Why have numbers fluctuated so much? Societal upheavals in the 1960s and changes in the church after Vatican II are often cited as a cause for the decrease in numbers. Analyses of these influences have been debated thoroughly, but one underreported change is the decline in the systems that in the past provided the formational background and basic education needed for acceptance into theologates. From 1967–68 to the present, high school seminaries almost totally disappeared, and students enrolled in them have dropped from 15,823 to 388. During the same period many college seminaries closed, and the number of freestanding and collaborative college seminaries dropped from 100 to 29; the number of college seminarians shrank from 13,401 to 1,416. For many years these contractions signaled the need for other sources of recruitment, but they have had limited success.

After the high point in 1967–68, the number of seminarians studying theology declined to a low point thirty years later in 1997–98. While

---

[2] See commentary by Thomas Walters, "Generational Differences: A Crucial Key."

numbers have fluctuated in the intervening years, the past five years have shown increases to pre-1990 levels (see table 4.1).[3] The relatively small current increases are attributed to the influence of recent popes and to more active recruitment of seminarians from other countries. Vocation offices are also becoming more adept at using modern technology to reach potential candidates. These factors no doubt have an effect, but it is also notable that the rates of decline and recovery are vastly different for diocesan candidates whose numbers have risen and religious candidates whose numbers continue to decline. Moreover, the positive change is tempered by the fact that since 1980, the introduction of pre-theology programs primarily in diocesan seminaries has added an average of 821 students annually to overall enrollment, compared to 641 added in each of the previous six years. This almost neutralizes the apparent gains. However the data is read, the fact remains that, for the past twenty years, there have been barely five hundred ordinations each year. This poses a significant challenge when considering the pastoral need of a Catholic population that has increased from 47 to 71 million since 1967.

Table 4.1

Seminarians in Theologates, 1967–2015

	Diocesan	*Religious*	*Total*
1967–68	4,876	3,283	8,159
1997–98	2,343	771	3,114
2014–15	2,799	851	3,650

An important explanation for the declining numbers of seminarians that should be highlighted relates to more stringent admissions requirements published in *PPF* V in 2005. The expanded norms call for a thorough screening process with more clearly defined parameters for those who are admitted, including attention to the differences in candidates based

---

[3] To avoid the idiosyncrasies of yearly shifts, another approach is to examine the changes by five-year averages. Beginning with the earliest data, 1967–72 in comparison with 2010–15, the number of seminarians in theologates is now 49 percent of the earlier years; diocesan numbers are 62 percent and religious 29 percent. The decline in colleges and high schools is even greater: the total for colleges is now 12 percent of the 1967–72 total; for high schools it is less than 4 percent.

Table 4.2

Age Distribution of Seminarians

Years	< 30 Number	Percent	30–39 Number	Percent	> 40 Number	Percent	TOTAL
1997–2000	4,707	47	3,657	37	1,530	15	9,932
2000–2005	7,064	41	6,774	40	3,272	19	17,074
2005–2010	8,328	50	5,207	31	3,171	19	16,074
2010–2015	9,847	54	5,639	31	2,855	16	18,306

on age, racial and ethnic backgrounds, and the requirement of being free of impediments of all types. More emphasis was accorded to psychological assessment, with strict guidelines for administering the tests (*PPF* V 51–53).[4] Additional norms disqualified an applicant with any evidence of or inclination toward criminal sexual activity with a minor. In spite of these more complete and explicit requirements, admissions committees have noted the frequent requests for exceptions to the norms from bishops and vocation directors, particularly norms related to academic background and the history of enrollment in other seminaries.

Age profiles. Data on the ages of seminarians, available since 1997–98, show a shift in directions (see table 4.2). In that year, 13 percent (405) of seminarians were over 40.

Before that time, the average age of the newly ordained was under 30, indicating that relatively few ordinands were older. Since then, due to an increase in the enrollment of older seminarians, the age of ordination climbed to over 35. By 1999–2000 the proportion of seminarians over 40 increased to 17 percent (590), and the highest proportion, 21 percent (694), occurred in the years 2004–06. In 2014–15, the proportion dropped back to 13 percent (475). The cause of the decrease is twofold: the population of older men seeking priesthood may be exhausted and vocation directors may be focusing their attention on younger men who will serve in active ministry for a longer time.[5]

---

[4] Since the publication of *PPF* V in 2005, *Guidelines for the Use of Psychology in Seminary Admissions* was published by the USCCB. The 2015 document provides extensive directives for psychologists on the purposes and components of assessments for admission and their use by seminary personnel in the formation process.

[5] Yet, an extensive survey that I conducted in 2011 of men who were ordained when they were older—from Sacred Heart Seminary and School of Theology and

Correspondingly, the proportion of seminarians under 30 averaged about 47 percent until 1998–99 when it began to drop steadily to 40 percent from 2001 to 2003. Beginning in 2004–5, the proportion under 30 climbed from 44 percent to an average of 50 percent for the next five years. By 2014–15 it reached 56 percent under 30 years old, the highest proportion since age data was collected. Adding to the directional shift, the proportion of seminarians ages 30–39 dropped by 9 percent from a high of 40 percent in 2000–2005 to 31 percent in 2014–15. During the most recent five-year period, the under-30 group averaged almost 2,000 per year (54 percent), ensuring that the ordination age will drop proportionately in the next few years. At the same time the Catholic population is growing older as fewer younger Catholics are practicing their faith. The vast age differences, and therefore ecclesial experiences, between the recently ordained and the majority of parishioners is likely to contribute even more to reported tension between the two groups in many parishes.

Racial and ethnic diversity. The racial and ethnic diversity among semi-narians has increased significantly since the early data was collected and is one of the most salient features of the profile. From 1994–95 to 2014–15, Caucasians dropped from a high of 86 percent to 64 percent; Hispanics/Latinos nearly doubled from 8 to 15 percent, African Americans remained stable at 4 percent, and Asians at about 10 percent. The Asian proportion has dropped slightly in theologates since its high point of 12 percent in 2008–9, while at the college level, the percentage of seminarians from Asian backgrounds has dropped by half from 12 percent in the early 2000s to 6 percent in recent years. A likely explanation is that young Vietnamese men of college age—second or even third generation Americans—have weaker ties to the faith than previous generations and are more likely to pursue other careers. The five-year averages indicate a relatively stable pattern in racial/ethnic proportions (see table 4.3) since 2000. The shift to a more diverse pool of seminarians since the 1990s is evident, but the nature of the diversity does not correspond to the diversity of church membership in that it underrepresents Hispanics/Latinos and overrepresents Caucasians. In light of the expected growth in the number of Hispanic/

Blessed (now St.) John XXIII National Seminary—revealed that they provided long years of service that was highly valued by their bishops. Thus, if fewer older men are now enrolling in seminaries, it seems more likely that the cause is unrelated to the performance of those who preceded them and, rather simply, to the lack of interest of older men in pursuing a priestly vocation.

Table 4.3

Racial and Ethnic Background of Seminarians

Year[6]	White/ Anglo/ Caucasian (%)	Black/ African American (%)	Hispanic/ Latino (%)	Asian/ Pacific Islander (%)	Other (%)
1993–2000	78	3	11	8	1
2000–2005	66	5	14	11	4
2005–2010	63	4	15	11	7
2010–2015	64	4	15	10	7

Latino/a Catholics, the question is whether or not the number of seminarians from Latino ethnic groups will expand as well.

Place of birth. Data on foreign-born seminarians has taken on great importance in recent years as the number of American-born seminarians has declined. According to CARA, from 1999 to 2015 the total number of seminarians coming from other countries was 12,777; the average per year was 799, which amounts to 23 percent of all seminarians. In the early years, the proportion of foreign-born to American-born seminarians was about 20 percent, but it peaked in 2009–10 at almost 28 percent. During 2014–15 the proportion dropped to 22 percent and averaged just under 800 (see table 4.4).[7]

Table 4.4

Foreign-Born Seminarians

	Total	Average # per year	Average % per year
2000–2005	17,074	3,415	20.5
2005–2010	16,706	3,341	24.9
2010–2015	18,306	3,661	23.5

[6] The first year data was collected was 1993–94; data is not available for 1995–96. Beginning in 2011–12, the category of "other" included Native Americans, multi-racial, and international students who do not identify with these racial and ethnic categories.

[7] The first year the data was collected on the place of birth of seminarians was in 1999–2000, when the number was 3,474 (23.8 percent).

Each year since 1999, seminarians from outside the United States have come from about eighty countries, but only since 2011 have countries of origin been identified. Consistently, the highest proportion of students grew up in Mexico, followed by Colombia and Vietnam, then the Philippines, Poland, and Nigeria. These six countries provided 60 percent of all foreign-born seminarians. Most enroll in American seminaries with the intent of serving as priests in this country. Since 2000, 83 percent of those ordained have remained in the United States—61 percent in dioceses and 22 percent in religious orders. The other 17 percent returned to their country of origin (all data from CARA Ministry reports for the years cited). The retention rate during seminary is reported to be slightly higher for international students than native born. During the same years, by adding the number of priests already ordained coming from other countries to the number of seminarians, an increasingly diverse presbyterate is evolving. It is estimated that a third of priests serving in this country will be from other countries within the next two decades.

The survey of rectors included several questions about international students, suggesting that many formation issues are unique to them. For the past ten years, nearly a quarter of seminarians have come from other countries and almost every theologate enrolls a sizeable proportion of them (only two report none). Two issues stand out: difficulty adjusting to the American ecclesial culture and learning English well enough to study theology and communicate effectively in speaking and writing. The pastoral reality of the church in the United States differs greatly from their previous experiences. Working with women, clericalism in the home culture, and relating well to Anglo students were among the concerns. The lack of preparation in English and the inability to be understood because of heavy accents also created problems. One rector addressed the issue as follows:

> We would hope that dioceses would provide such seminarians with at least a full propaedeutic year which includes intensive English language studies, but that is not always the case. We would also prefer that during that year or in some other context they have at least a full year living and functioning in a U.S. parish in some way. The cultural challenges for these seminarians are enormous, and we do what we can to provide remedial services during their formation.

Rectors report that adjusting to all of these cultural differences requires significant time and attention from formation advisers since concerns about the cultural environment in general present notable challenges.[8]

Table 4.5

Lay Students Enrolled in Theologates

Years	Average # Degree-seeking	Average # Certificate	Program Not Specified[9]	Average Total
1994–1998	1,349	114	1,036	2,498
1998–2003	1,903	103	1,407	3,413
2004–2009	1,996	623	--	2,619
2010–2015	2,112	893	--	3,005

B. Lay Ecclesial Ministry Students

Numbers. Some information is available about lay students studying in theologates where seminarians are also enrolled, but it is not as long-standing or detailed as it is for seminarians. By 1975, just a few years after theologates began accepting lay students, the enrollment was 1,393; ten years later the number was 2,902. Since 1994–95, data has been published every two years (see table 4.5). From 1994 to 2015, the average enrollment of lay students was 2,919, with the high point in 2002–3 at 3,682 and the low point in 2008–9 at 2,359. One of the main reasons attributed to the decline in numbers between 2004–5 and 2010–11 was the reduction in financial support for lay students from dioceses following the clergy sexual abuse crisis.[10] The two most recent surveys, from 2012 to

---

[8] Katarina Schuth, "Fully Understanding the Moment and Embracing the Future: Seminary and Religious Candidates," in *To Be One in Christ: Intercultural Formation and Ministry*, ed. Fernando Ortiz and Gerard McGlone, SJ, 35–55 (Collegeville, MN: Liturgical Press, 2015).

[9] It is important to note that in earlier years some theologates did not differentiate between degree-seeking and certificate students.

[10] Another consequence of the reduction in diocesan resources available for education was the drop in the number of diocesan-sponsored lay ecclesial ministry formation programs, which from 1999 through 2003 averaged 320 to less than 200 in recent years. The number of students enrolled in those programs dropped from over 36,048 in 2002

2015, show a recovery in numbers to an average of 3,176 in those years. Rectors reported that the seminaries' ability to provide financial aid was a key element in their decision to enroll. Other factors were the quality of programs, reputation of the school, and a welcoming environment. An active marketing effort in some schools is also responsible for success in encouraging their enrollment.

Since 2010, the nine religious order schools on average enrolled 38 percent of lay students seeking a degree. In part responding to cutbacks in diocesan-sponsored programs, all theologates but nine now offer certificate programs, most of them fairly new. In diocesan theologates, 40 percent of their lay students are seeking certificates, which amounts to 85 percent of all certificate students. Correspondingly, religious order theologates enroll 15 percent of certificate students. All in all, current students are more likely to be pursuing certificates in diocesan schools and are more likely to be seeking degrees in religious order schools.

C. Characteristics of All Lay Ministry Students

The data concerning age, racial and ethnic background, and vocational status has been reported since 1997 for *all* lay ecclesial ministry students, regardless of the type of institution in which they were enrolled. The data is not divided according to students enrolled in religious order theologates or in diocesan programs or colleges and universities.[11] Knowing about this larger population is useful in analyzing the 15 percent enrolled in theologates.

Vocational status of all lay ministry students. From 1997–98 to 2014–15, the proportion of laywomen students in all institutions fluctuated from

---

to an average of 18,146 from 2004 to 2012. Since then the numbers have grown to an average of 22,500, related in part to the availability of positions due to the retirement of many lay ecclesial ministers who were among the first to be hired in their positions in the mid to late 1970s.

[11] CARA does not divide data on lay students according to degree and certificate programs for all institutions; however, of all ministry degree candidates, the larger theologates—those with more than 100 lay students—enroll 40 percent of them. A much smaller proportion, about 20 percent, receive certificates in theologates. Apart from total enrollment, other data on lay students are combined with those studying in colleges and universities, as well as in diocesan programs. About 60 percent of lay students attend colleges and universities to earn degrees, and a higher proportion enroll in diocesan formation programs to earn certificates.

about 58 percent in the early years, to 63 percent in the middle years, and recently back to 58 percent. In comparable years, the proportion of lay-men increased steadily from about 30 percent to 33 percent to 38 percent. The small remaining percentage includes a declining number of women religious, now about 2 percent, and a few others, among them permanent deacons, religious brothers, and non-Catholics whose vocational status is not listed. Details based on three sample years from 2008 to the present show that the proportions enrolled in *theologates-only* are highest for lay-women with about 40 percent and second for laymen at 25 percent, but in contrast to laywomen, laymen are more likely to be seeking degrees than certificates. The proportion of women religious is higher in theologates than in diocesan programs at nearly 10 percent, and the vast majority of them are seeking degrees. The vocational status is not identified for about 25 percent of the students.

Racial and ethnic backgrounds of all lay ministry students. Taking into account all of these lay students, their backgrounds have changed drama-tically since 1997. The main differences are as follows:

- From 1997 to 2007, more than 70 percent were Caucasian, a propor-tion that dropped to 49 percent by 2011; since then it has declined to a low of 43 percent.

- The reverse has been true for Latino/a enrollment, which hovered around 20 percent from 1997 until 2008; after that it was in the 30 percent range, and since 2011 the average is 46 percent.

- Three ethnic categories—African American, Asian American, and other—have each remained around 3 percent since data was first collected.

This information shows a high proportion of Hispanic/Latino/a lay stu-dents preparing for ministry, comparable to but slightly higher than their proportion of the total Catholic population, and unlike the lower pro-portion of Hispanic/Latino seminarians. Many of these lay students are enrolled in diocesan certificate programs. Asian American lay students show a relatively low proportion at 3 percent compared to seminarians at 10 percent. Keeping in mind that this data is for all lay students pre-paring for ministry, not just those studying in theologates, the shift of most consequence is the decline in the proportion of Caucasian students. The racial and ethnic distribution of lay ministry students more closely matches the Catholic population as a whole and brings to light the continued imbalance in the seminarian proportions relative to all Catholics.[12]

Table 4.6

Age Distribution of All Lay Ministry Students

Years	% under 30	% 30–39	% 40–49	% 50–59	% 60 and over
1997–2000	8	21	34	26	11
2000–2005	9	18	33	29	12
2005–2010	11	18	30	29	12
2010–2015	14	19	30	25	12

Age distribution of all lay ministry students. Just as with the ethnic and racial numbers, the ages of lay students include all those preparing for ministry. In the earliest years for which data is available, from 1997 to 2006, about 8 percent were under 30 years of age. Since then the average under 30 is about 12 percent. As with racial and ethnic data, ages of students are reported only for all lay ministry students (see table 4.6). Without a doubt, the average ages of those enrolled in theologates-only, especially in degree programs, is considerably younger than for all enrollees. The proportion of those over 50, for example, would drop from about 37 percent to 1 or 2 percent. Those under 30 would be a considerably higher proportion of lay students in theologates. Similar to seminarian ages, the group under 30 has grown slightly, but does not approach the high proportion of the youngest seminarians, which in the most recent five years has averaged 54 percent.

Implications of Characteristics of Seminarians and Lay Ministry Students

Considered in the aggregate, those who minister in the future possess characteristics vastly different from those of current ministers, both ordained and lay. Many facts about seminarians have shifted in significant

---

[12] The racial and ethnic data for seminarians is considerably different: Caucasian seminarians are still on average 63 percent (43 percent for lay students), Hispanic/Latino/as about 15 percent (45 percent for lay students), Asian Americans 10 percent (3 percent for lay students), and African Americans 4 percent (3 percent for lay students). Other seminarians are 7 percent (3 percent for lay students).

ways. Foremost is the drastic decline in numbers, then in age profiles, and finally in racial and ethnic backgrounds that are affected by the presence of both American and international students. Accounting for lay ministry students studying in theologates is a more recent endeavor and detailed data is not as complete, but certain factors are observable. In many ways, the statistics clearly demonstrate the divergence between the characteristics of these two groups of students, which are likely to have consequences for their relationships in ministering together. These are the following: more priests who are younger in contrast to older lay ministers, more Caucasian priests alongside multiethnic lay ministers, and proportionately fewer priests than lay ministers. Moreover, as priests and lay ministers are reaching retirement age in high numbers, the replacement rate of both is decidedly inadequate. The implications of these differences are acute for parish, diocesan, and institutional ministry in the future as they seek to hire well-prepared staffs.

Since the projected number of future priests and ministers is modest, especially in light of the growing Catholic population, it is more imperative than ever that the men and women now preparing for ministry learn to collaborate. Yet, in recent years especially in diocesan seminaries, lay programs have been separated from seminarian programs. The full consequences of this division are not yet realized for current students, but past studies point to potential problems. Through the early 2000s, extensive surveys on the views and attitudes of seminarians showed their increasing proclivity to see themselves set apart in future ministry from those who are not ordained. More recently, these findings were supplemented by studies of those who had been ordained five to nine years, and priests ordained from Vatican II to the new century.[13] This research compared young priests with older priests—reflecting generational changes and shifts in their perspectives. A well-known characterization describes older priests as exemplifying the servant-leader model and younger priests as representing the cultic model. Specific characteristics that demonstrate the

---

[13] Among them were three comprehensive studies published between 2002 and 2006, two by Dean Hoge and a third coauthored with Jacqueline Wenger: Hoge, *The First Five Years of the Priesthood: A Study of Newly Ordained Catholic Priests* (Collegeville, MN: Liturgical Press, 2002) and *Experiences of Priests Ordained Five to Nine Years: A Study of Recently Ordained Catholic Priests* (Arlington, VA: NCEA, 2006); and Hoge and Wenger, *Evolving Visions of the Priesthood: Changes from Vatican II to the Turn of the New Century* (Collegeville, MN: Liturgical Press, 2003).

contrast are: (1) the priest as pastoral leader vs. "man set apart"; (2) attitude toward church magisterium as valuing flexible structure vs. valuing strict hierarchy; (3) in liturgy and devotions, allowing for flexibility vs. following established rules; (4) on theological perspective, allowing for theological differences vs. defending "orthodoxy"; and (5) on attitude toward celibacy, being optional for the priesthood vs. seen as essential to the priesthood.[14] These studies about priests conceivably reflect an image of what they were like as seminarians, demonstrating how many changes have come about in the past thirty years or so.

A separate evolution is evident among lay ecclesial ministers, many of whom are serving in roles performed by priests and religious in the past. Since they have become more educated and experienced and assume more responsibilities, they expect to be regarded as coworkers and partners, but this expectation is sometimes not compatible with the views of the newly ordained. As a consequence, when older pastors are replaced by priests with a different ecclesial understanding of the role of lay ministers, sometimes entire staffs are replaced. While the USCCB has provided solid pastoral guidance regarding the role of lay ecclesial ministers in their 2005 document, *Co-Workers in the Vineyard of the Lord*, it seems safe to say that few seminarians or priests have studied the document as a way of reframing how clergy are to work with their lay colleagues. As a result, what suffers is the steady work needed to learn how to be effective for the call to true collaboration in service to God's people.

---

[14] Paraphrasing from *Evolving Visions of the Priesthood*, the way the authors contrasted the older with the younger priests on these five characteristics, 114.

Chapter 5

Human and Spiritual Formation Developments

Introduction to Formation

The 2005 edition of the *PPF* for the first time identified four areas of formation for seminarians—human, spiritual, intellectual, and pastoral.[1] Both the order and terminology used to organize formation content changed from the first *PPF* edition in 1971 to the fifth edition in 2005. The earliest list included "The Academic Program," "Pastoral Formation," and "Spiritual Formation," with considerable emphasis on the academic. The second edition migrated the titles to "Development of the Seminarian: Personal and Spiritual," followed by "Academic and Pastoral"; the third edition remained unchanged. In the fourth edition, titles were simply "Spiritual," "Intellectual," and "Pastoral Formation." Only in 2005 were all four areas included, with human formation added to the three named in the fourth edition. Documents of both the universal and local church were influential in determining the development and content of programs, with the most comprehensive and direct descriptions found in *PPF* V.

---

[1] Originally, elements of formation were referred to as "pillars," but recently "areas" or "dimensions" are favored terms. This new nomenclature reflects the growing understanding of the importance of the relationships among the four areas rather than their being viewed as separate entities, so these newer terms will be used throughout the book.

The universal church document, *Pastores Dabo Vobis (PDV)*, was most important in defining the areas of formation, followed by *Ratio Fundamentalis*. From time to time directives are issued by the local church for a particular occasion or on a specific topic, such as the 2008 report of the Apostolic Visitation of the American seminaries and *Guidelines for the Use of Psychology in Seminary Admissions*, both related to clergy sexual abuse. These, too, are reflected in program requirements.

Furnished with these instructions, the boards, administrators, and faculty of theologates have developed programs according to distinctive local circumstances, the mixture of students, and the ecclesial viewpoint of decision makers. The unique character of each school and the level of involvement and knowledge of its leaders influence the variation in content and quality of programs. All areas of formation are required, regardless of where they are offered—in a single institution or divided between two institutions. A typical example of the first is a freestanding diocesan seminary, and of the second, a religious order school.[2] Common to all types of programs are efforts to identify the qualities students are expected to develop in each area of formation, to clarify the desired outcomes, and to assess the level of achievement.

While the content and format of formation have undergone development in the past thirty years, not all theologates have modified their programs to the same extent nor have they revised and developed the four areas in equal proportion. In the 1980s, many theologates enhanced pastoral formation, an element needing more emphasis as many seminarians were entering theology with little parish experience or pastoral ministry. The content and method of academic formation gained attention in the 1990s as the faculties had concern about the implications of the growing multicultural nature of the church. Not only were more seminarians coming from other countries and backgrounds, but parishes were growing in ethnic diversity and in the organization of ministries. The situation required more explicit instruction on the connection between theology

---

[2] Diocesan theologates, except for those whose students live in a separate house, are responsible for all aspects of formation and so they are more concerned about human and spiritual development than religious order theologates, whose seminarians usually live in the houses of formation of their congregation where human and spiritual formation is provided. In all types of theologates, lay student programs are based on the four areas of formation, but the content is distinctive. The types of theologates are described in detail in chapter 2 under "The Structures of Theologates."

and pastoral services.[3] Spiritual formation continued as a core element of formation, but it was affected by the call for development of a new category, human formation. Thus in the 2005 *PPF*, this dimension, based on the requirements specified in *PDV* by Pope John Paul II in 1992 and the revelation of widespread sexual abuse among clergy, received particular attention from 2002 onward.

Other influences shaping formation programs included

- variation in age, racial, and ethnic backgrounds of seminarians, including their ecclesial experiences;
- seminarians' limited understanding of the spiritual and human dimensions of formation and of church teaching in general;
- vastly different qualifications and ecclesial experiences of many faculty and administrators, who were rapidly replacing those of a previous generation; and
- ministry requirements and conditions that continue to be in flux due to the decreasing number of priests that result in assignments to multiple parishes and/or to a large parish with no other priests, which means serving exclusively with lay ministers.

The required modifications in all areas of formation have challenged the ingenuity of faculty when dealing with these issues for the first time or addressing them in greater depth. Moreover, coinciding with adaptations in priestly formation, formation for lay ministry students has expanded to meet their formational requirements.

A. Human Formation

The evolution of human formation began in earnest after the publication of *PDV*.[4] In an expansive description, John Paul II designated human formation as fundamental, the basis for all preparation for priesthood. He said, "The whole work of priestly formation would be deprived of

---

[3] Faculty attending the Keystone Conferences from 1996 to 2002 identified three areas that required attention—diversity, integration, and assessment—related to all areas of formation. Participants focused especially on academic preparation of seminarians, but also considered adaptations that would be effective for lay students.

[4] See commentary by Leon Hutton, "Human Formation: Fostering Happy, Healthy, and Holy Ministers to Be a Bridge to Christ in Service to God's People."

its necessary foundation if it lacked a suitable human formation" (*PDV* 43). He delineated a series of human qualities that are necessary for ministry, for example, being balanced in judgment and behavior, having the capacity to relate to others, demonstrating human maturity—especially the affective dimension, understanding sexuality in the context of celibate chastity, being generous and faithful to commitments, and possessing a moral conscience. The dilemma formators faced was determining how to properly reallocate to human formation some of the many topics previously covered under spiritual formation. The modifications have come slowly. Even more than twenty years after the call for change, theologates are still in the process of expanding and implementing this area as well as distinguishing it from spiritual formation.

The reasons for the prolonged period of adjustment may be related to the way earlier editions of the *PPF* handled the topics, that is, conflating "spiritual" and "personal" formation. Recent turnover in leadership in these areas has added to the problem, so some theologates have progressed at a slower rate in organizing changes. By 2015, among diocesan theologates responsible for these areas of formation, half (fifteen of thirty) had named "human formation" as a separate program. Another twelve (40 percent) still used dual titles: "formation" in general and "spiritual formation," and three theologates (10 percent) used only "formation" to cover both areas.[5] The directors of programs, assisted by many associate directors, hold titles consonant with the program titles in their institution.

The topics typically included in human formation are numerous and, though based on *PDV* as the common source, vary among theologates. To add to the confusion, many topics—such as celibacy, moral character, and virtues—have been covered in more than one aspect of formation where different editions of the *PPF* were applicable. Thus, careful discernment is needed to determine how to divide the material. The clearest example of the quandary is the treatment of celibacy, which has been handled very differently in both content and placement in the five editions of the *PPF*. It was initially covered under pastoral ministry, then in subsequent editions under personal and spiritual formation as one area, then under two separate areas of human and spiritual formation, and in the fifth edition

---

[5] Since religious order theologates do not usually provide the human and spiritual dimensions of formation, this discussion pertains solely to those in diocesan seminaries and the few separate residences for diocesan seminarians.

"preparation for celibacy is one of the primary aims of the human formation program of any seminary" (*PPF* V 90). The evolution of celibacy formation illustrates changing social and cultural awareness in the church and among formators. The defining moment for the recent changes arose largely from the sexual abuse crisis, but also reflected efforts to more fully incorporate the teaching of *PDV* on the topic.

Celibacy

The differences in length of presentation and points of emphasis are most notable between the first three editions of the *PPF* (1971, 1976, and 1981) and the last two (1992 and 2005).

- *In the first edition, 1971,* celibacy was treated in four short paragraphs mainly under the "Pastoral Ministry" section and described as deeply rooted in the Lord for the sake of the pastoral mission. Developing appropriate attitudes toward celibacy, sex, and love were mentioned, as well as proper relationships with women.

- *The second edition, 1976,* included five paragraphs on celibacy, under "Development of the Seminarian: Personal and Spiritual." The one new paragraph emphasized the personal value of celibacy as a way of sharing in the life of Christ.

- *In the third edition, 1981,* eleven paragraphs were about celibacy, five of which were very similar to the 1976 edition. Four new paragraphs, added under "Development of the Seminarian: Personal and Spiritual," treated topics such as the necessity of learning the value of celibacy in a consumer culture, understanding the nature of sexuality, including homosexuality, and the church's teachings on all these topics. It also discussed the call to celibacy, the expectations for behavior, and the necessity of evaluating proper attitudes toward celibacy. Two other new paragraphs, under the introduction "Priestly Formation in the U.S.A.," emphasized the obligatory nature of celibacy and the responsibility of the seminary to prepare students to live out their commitment to celibacy.

- *The fourth edition, 1992,* expands the length to thirty-three paragraphs, found largely under "Foundations of Priestly Formation: The Spiritual Life of Diocesan Priests," with a few paragraphs under "The Admission and Continuing Formation of Seminarians."

After describing the negative influences of the present social climate on lifelong commitment to celibacy, most of the content is directed toward spiritual goals, behavioral expectations, and admissions standards. With Jesus as the model of the celibate life, the program was to make clear the rationale of the church for requiring celibacy. The content was to focus on the essential meaning of celibacy, its value, and its relationship to Christ, church, and ordination. Necessary practices to live a celibate life were mentioned, including virtues and habits and seeing Mary as a model and support. Eight paragraphs focused on "Celibacy for the Kingdom" and "Priestly Life and Ministry: Witness to the Kingdom." Psychological assessment relative to celibacy in the admissions process was seen as integral.

- *The fifth edition, 2005,* changes substantially from the fourth and includes twenty-three paragraphs specifically concerning celibate chastity. The material was expanded and incorporated under a new lengthy section on "Human Formation," based on *PDV.* It spoke of integrating human formation with all other aspects of formation and provided extensive norms on "Preparation for Celibacy." A detailed explanation of basic attitudes and behavioral expectations of celibacy was presented along with guidelines for how to understand and accept the value of one's sexuality when directed to God's service.

The program was designed to foster growth in solid moral character and moral conscience, to help seminarians develop habits and skills to live a celibate commitment, and to understand the meaning of chastity. Several topics were mentioned for the first time in this edition:

- disqualification for admission if any criminal sexual activity with a minor or inclination toward such was known;
- the necessity of following guidelines of the Holy See regarding same-sex experience and/or inclinations; and
- the requirement to investigate certain conditions prior to orders, such as whether or not the candidate had been sexually abused and whether any remedies were needed.

The fifth edition of the *PPF* urged high standards and vigilance pertaining to sexuality, affective maturity, and capacity to live celibate chastity. It expanded norms for admission of candidates, naming psychosexual development, capacity to live a life of celibacy, and a minimum of two years of continent living before entry. The document recognized the importance of awareness of sexual abuse by clergy from 2002 onward. This single topic was the major facet of program development in human formation, but receives less attention throughout the rest of the document.

Other Aspects of Human Formation Programs

Topics typically covered in human formation programs, in addition to celibacy, are numerous. Most programs sequence the elements according to the number of years seminarians have been enrolled in theologates. The earlier years focus on development of suitable personal qualities and later on, as they approach ordination, on characteristics that demonstrate the human qualities needed to minister effectively. Formation faculty commonly group elements according to topics such as health and well-being, pastoral requirements, and virtues. In the first instance, physical and psychological health take into account respect and care for the body and emotional maturity. The test is to see if the seminarian can balance the demands of prayer, study, service, and recreation during formation so that he can handle the pressures of ministry effectively after ordination. Seminarians are expected to be approachable in relationships and inter-actions, demonstrate self-confidence without being arrogant, and show an interest in and concern for others. Formation directors expect them to be open and honest in one-on-one and group conversations as they develop an awareness of the effects of their demeanor.

As they progress through the program, more attention is focused on their becoming public persons with high moral standards and capacity to lead. Their words, behaviors, and body language need to be consistent with priesthood, under particular scrutiny since sexual abuse has been in the forefront. They are expected to grow in sensitivity to the needs and aspirations of others, be open to new viewpoints, and engage with people who are of a different race, ethnicity, sex, economic class, personality, and ideology. They must have suitable work habits that give evidence of leader-ship ability and a collaborative spirit. In a sense, all aspects of formation are responsible for development of virtues related to ministry, such as being compassionate, generous, prudent and consistent in judgments, authentic, and insightful. However, it is the responsibility of human formation directors to assure that these and other qualities are present.

B. Spiritual Formation

Pope John Paul II differentiated spiritual formation and human formation in *PDV*, and at the same time he clearly indicated the connection between the two: human formation finds its completion in spiritual formation by bringing the full truth of oneself to God, living a celibate life in the social and cultural situations of the present day, and giving oneself generously and freely in pastoral ministry. The development of the spiritual life is presented with reference to *OT*: "Spiritual formation . . . should be conducted in such a way that the students may learn to live in intimate and unceasing union with God the Father through his Son Jesus Christ, in the Holy Spirit" (*PDV* 45). The meaning of this broad exhortation is clarified: seminarians should faithfully meditate on the word of God, actively participate in the Eucharist and the Divine Office, and show reverence and love for the Blessed Virgin Mary. After a detailed description of required spiritual practices, the second admonition is to seek Christ in people. It is at this point that *PDV* connects spiritual formation to celibate living. Priests are to devote themselves to pastoral ministry with undivided love for people by living a celibate life and instructing the faithful on pastoral reasons for it (*PDV* 49). In summary, spiritual formation is to include the requisite spiritual practices that will lead to seeking Christ in the people and to prepare seminarians to "love and live celibacy according to its true nature and its real purposes, that is, for evangelical, spiritual and pastoral motives" (*PDV* 50).

The importance of spiritual formation is unmistakable in the way it is presented in *PPF* V: it is "the core which unifies and gives life to his *being* a priest and his *acting* as a priest" (*PDV* 45) and is intended to be comprehensive in nature. The introduction repeats the mandate of *PDV* about living in intimate and unceasing union with the Trinity, which is to be "far more than a personal or individual relationship with the Lord; it is also a communion with the Church, which is his body" (*PPF* V 108). The breadth of the mandate is expressed in the variety of practices and characteristics that are to foster spiritual growth. The list of practices includes

- sacramental and liturgical practices, such as Holy Eucharist, Liturgy of the Hours, and the sacrament of penance;

- reading the Bible and reflecting daily on the Sacred Scriptures;

- other prayer-related practices, such as personal meditation, devotions, and retreats and days of recollection; and

- spiritual direction, needed for growth in sanctity, virtue, and readiness for holy orders.

Certain characteristics that should be cultivated through spiritual formation are highlighted: celibacy as a commitment to a way of life; simplicity
of life; solidarity; solitude; asceticism and penance; and reconciliation
fostering peacemaking, a nonviolent way of life, and a reconciling spirit.
Other expectations of spiritual formation address the apostolic dimensions
of the priesthood and ongoing spiritual formation by establishing attitudes,
habits, and practices that will continue after ordination.

Translating these admirable goals into an effective program is a challenge for formation personnel. They have designed a wide array of formats
and chosen a broad range of content, seeking to adapt them to the situation
of their students while taking into account their personnel and resources.
One of the challenges in dealing with spiritual formation is evaluating
its effectiveness, an accountability measured by participation in spiritual
exercises and their growth as men of faith (*PPF* V 280). Toward this end, a
task force developed *An Assessment Workbook*, offering ways of measuring
external practices without violating the internal forum.[6] Examples of measurable criteria would be that students participate daily in the Eucharist
and pray the Liturgy of the Hours, receive spiritual direction on a regular
basis, engage in devotional prayer, demonstrate a habit of obedience to
legitimate ecclesial authority, and welcome and respond knowledgably to
questions of faith. While some of the outcomes of spiritual formation
are similar to human formation, the approaches and rationale are distinct.

C. Concepts Common to Human and Spiritual Formation

Formats Used to Address Topics

Various ways of delivering formation content are employed by faculty, some in group settings and others individually. Depending on the
size of the student body and the nature of the material, at least six types
of groups are used to convey concepts and attitudes. Conferences by the
rector are often directed to the entire student body and tend to cover

---

[6] A collaboration between the NCEA Seminary Department and the ATS Commission on Accrediting, under the leadership of Msgr. Jeremiah McCarthy and Rev.
Mark Latcovich. Preliminary text published in 2014, publication forthcoming by ATS.

topics about prayer and the spiritual life, as well as the overall meaning of commitment to the priesthood. If a particularly problematic issue arises, the rector may take the lead in identifying the concern and presenting it. Faculty follow through in smaller groups or individual sessions to address the specifics. Other occasions call for all-school conferences led by guest speakers who speak on the spiritual life and pastoral engagement or who have comprehensive expertise on sensitive matters. Recently, for instance, psychologists, legal experts, and social workers have been called on due to concerns about child sexual abuse by clergy. When material is developmental in nature, building from year-to-year, instruction is presented to class groups in conferences, workshops, and academic courses. Even smaller support groups are formed for faith sharing and discussion of issues of human development, such as celibacy, affective maturity, and leadership. Besides the group contexts, several forms of individual human and spiritual formation are provided, including required spiritual direction formation advising, as well as counseling, which may be optional or mandatory for some students.[7]

The roles of and requirements for spiritual directors and formation advisors have evolved over the past thirty years.[8] Spiritual directors describe their role as one that supports the seminarian in discerning his call to the priesthood and in reaching a deeper, personal level of relationship with God in prayer. They emphasize the importance of his coming to a profound self-understanding that enables him to embrace a decision for celibacy with freedom and maturity. Especially since the sexual abuse crisis, many directors report that they focus on moral virtues that will foster a commitment to celibate chastity. The relationship between the director and the seminarian is confidential,[9] but directors advise their directees

---

[7] Academic advising is universally provided, but it may be given in small groups or individually, depending on the needs of the student and the custom in the theologate.

[8] The 1988 report of the apostolic visitation of all US seminaries authorized in 1981 and coordinated by Bishop John Marshall of Burlington, VT, mandated that spiritual directors for seminarians be priests. Following the 2008 report of the Apostolic Visitation of seminaries begun in 2005, formation advising also was to be provided only by priests.

[9] The nature of this relationship is defined in *PPF* V 134: "Disclosures that a seminarian makes in the course of spiritual direction belong to the internal forum. Consequently, the spiritual director is held to the strictest confidentiality concerning information received in spiritual direction. He may neither reveal it nor use it. [See CIC, c. 240§2; CCEO, c. 339§3.] The only possible exception to this standard of

to bring to the attention of their formation advisors matters that need attention in the external forum.

Formation advisers, sometimes called mentors or directors, have a more expansive role in that they are to discuss and provide guidance in all matters that pertain to preparation for priesthood. They are to review all areas of formation—human, spiritual, intellectual, and pastoral—but considerable attention is given to human and spiritual formation since most theologates also assign academic advisers and pastoral supervisors. It is the responsibility of the formation advisers to bring to the attention of the rector any concerns about the seminarian that might be detrimental to the church, especially regarding celibacy and the capacity to live a chaste life. Formation advisors discuss issues such as friendships, relationships with women, how to handle loneliness and solitude, and personality or character traits that are counter-indicative for the celibate life. Other virtues and qualities necessary for successful ministry are to be taken into account as well.

Results of Changes in Human and Spiritual Formation

The new and renewed emphasis on these two areas of formation have created stronger programs in many ways but also have raised issues, especially for diocesan seminaries. The major change of introducing a separate program for human formation has led administrators to allot substantial resources to develop this critical area. After reviewing the complexity of the prescribed content, some theologates have arranged workshops and educational opportunities for faculty who will be responsible for the program. Besides knowledge, faculty who have extended pastoral and seminary formation experience have been able to develop comprehensive and integrated programs.

About half the schools have adapted their administrative structures by adding a new department with a director of human formation and associates in proportion to the number of students. When program configurations change, those responsible for the implementation need to be aware of several possible concerns:

---

confidentiality would be the case of grave, immediate, or mortal danger involving the directee or another person." If spiritual direction coincides with the celebration of the sacrament of penance, then the absolute strictures of the seal of confession hold, and no information may be revealed or used.

- Both human and spiritual formation cover the development of similar virtues and qualities, especially on issues related to celibacy. Careful coordination between the two departments is essential to be sure that all topics are covered without excessive duplication.

- The relatively new approaches and some new content require on-going education for those who have major responsibility for formation advising. The many faculty who are recently appointed and relatively inexperienced in seminary work may not have had the opportunity for intensive preparation, or they may feel they do not need it. Students can be shortchanged if the faculty as a whole is not prepared for the changes.[10]

- Priest faculty in most diocesan seminaries have acquired additional formation advising responsibilities because in the past lay faculty and women religious also served as advisers. Since they no longer continue in the role, priests must take on more seminarian advisees along with teaching and, in some cases, providing spiritual direction.

- The internal (confidential) forum and the external (public or open) forum must be clearly separated. Establishing two distinct departments can be a helpful means of ensuring this division, but at the same time the departments must cooperate so that integration can occur. On the part of seminarians, difficulty can arise if they fail to see the connections between the human and spiritual dimensions of their formation or if they experience the relationship with two directors as either unrelated or unnecessarily repetitious.

When administrators and faculty give full attention to these areas of formation, the desired outcomes of human and spiritual formation are attained. The prescribed changes have the potential of preparing seminarians more thoroughly and successfully for the complex ministries they will provide.

---

[10] According to the rectors' survey, less than half of human and spiritual formation personnel participate frequently in ongoing formation. Their complaint is the lack of availability of programs that are suited to their needs. The Institute for Pastoral Formation is used more than other programs (16), but some do not find that this program meets their needs. Often spiritual directors are priests who are working in parishes or ministries other than seminaries and so they do not have the time, or perhaps perceived need, for further education.

Chapter 6

Intellectual and Pastoral Formation Programs

Introduction

Intellectual and pastoral preparation are integral dimensions of formation for priesthood candidates and students preparing for lay ecclesial ministry. *OT*, the 1965 Vatican II document on seminary education, highlighted the importance of integrating all areas of formation, a theme that permeates the five editions of the *PPF*.[1] This directive is supplemented by giving special attention to pastoral formation:

> All four pillars of formation are interwoven and go forward concurrently. Still, in a certain sense, pastoral formation is the culmination of the entire formation process: "The whole formation imparted to candidates for the priesthood aims at preparing them to enter into communion with the charity of Christ the Good Shepherd. Hence, their formation in its different aspects must have a fundamentally pastoral character."[2]

PDV introduces the term "intellectual formation," which was commonly referred to as academic formation before 1992. The purposes of intellec-

---

[1] As noted earlier, the term "pillars" has been used to identify the various aspects of formation. More recently, the terms "areas" or "dimensions" are used to move away from the image of stand-alone or separate parts.

[2] Quoting *PDV* 57, the goal of formation as pastoral is reinforced in *PPF* V 236.

tual formation are outlined in *PPF* V 164. These include a comprehensive understanding of the mysteries of the Catholic faith, an ability to explain and defend the reasoning that supports the faith, and an aptitude to contemplate, share, and communicate the mysteries of faith to others. This movement from knowledge to application describes an essentially pastoral orientation and brings together all areas of formation. The status of intellectual formation has varied over time. It enjoyed an assumption of deep-seated commitment until the mid-1980s. Shortly before Vatican II, some prominent seminary leaders complained about the deterioration of intellectual requirements, but the issue was not examined in depth until later. By the time Pope John Paul II wrote *PDV* in 1992, the commitment to academics had eroded perceptibly:

> It is necessary to oppose firmly the tendency to play down the seriousness of studies and the commitment to them. This tendency is showing itself in certain spheres of the Church, also as a consequence of the insufficient and defective basic education of students beginning the philosophical and theological curriculum. The very situation of the Church today demands increasingly that teachers be truly able to face the complexity of the times and that they be in a position to face competently, with clarity and deep reasoning, the questions about meaning which are put by the people of today, questions which can only receive full and definitive reply in the Gospel of Jesus Christ. (*PDV* 56)

Does the academic program in theologates, including the pastoral dimension, adequately prepare seminarians for ministry? The survey responses of rectors/presidents indicate that two-thirds of them are quite satisfied that it does. Most agree that the number of credits required for a degree is about right, 30 percent believe it is too extensive, and only one says it does not require enough. When asked if the pressures of a four-year program are too great, three-fourths responded they are not, but one-fourth (all diocesan rectors) believe there is too much pressure. The solution to the problem, they say, is to reduce the number of credits, lengthen the program, or restructure it with shorter breaks and more time in session. For the most part the rectors/presidents believe the *PPF* requirements are good and necessary, but they want faculty to more effectively integrate the course content from different disciplines as well as integrate all four areas of formation. A number of respondents favor adjusting the length of the program according to individual backgrounds of students. All who find the academic requirements too burdensome have been in office less than five years, and several of them are concerned that not enough time is allowed for leisure and contemplation. This view is related to concerns expressed in *PDV* about downplaying academics and to comments voiced by deans and faculty during interviews. It represents an emerging controversy about allotment of time and effort among the four areas of formation, intensified by the introduction of significant new requirements in human formation.

A. Intellectual Formation

Program Expansion and Curricular Content

Since the mid-1980s, theologates have introduced numerous new degree programs in hopes of attracting more students and in response to calls to prepare more lay students to fill increasingly specialized ministerial roles. The curricular content of degree programs has changed in response to some church directives, especially those found in the five editions of the *PPF* and in *Co-Workers in the Vineyard of the Lord*. The documents seek to respond pastorally to the changing demographics of church membership, structural and personnel changes in parishes and dioceses, and the needs of Catholics living in contemporary society. These concerns and the challenges of the new evangelization they reflect require integrating the pastoral goal with all aspects of intellectual formation. In response, theologates to some degree have adapted their programs and courses for a more effective response, but much remains to be accomplished.

Degree Programs and Special Studies

The vast majority of theologates have expanded their offerings in the past thirty years in response to the needs of the church and in hope of increasing enrollment. The basic degree for seminarians continues to be the MDiv. Most schools also offer master-level degrees mainly for lay students in areas such as pastoral ministry, pastoral studies, and religious education. Some also offer doctor of ministry degrees for experienced ministers. Academic masters degrees are available for all students; seminarians sometimes combine them with the MDiv. A few of the university-related theologates offer doctoral degrees (STD and PhD) as well. Six schools have credentialed faculty to offer pontifical degrees on their own; another eight offer the bachelor in sacred theology (STB) and the licentiate in sacred theology (STL) through affiliation with another institution that has an ecclesiastical faculty. Several more schools are exploring the possibility of adding these degrees.

Among numerous special programs are biblical studies, Catholic-Jewish-Muslim studies, Hispanic ministry, and homiletics in addition to pre-theology, permanent deacon, certificate, and sabbatical programs. While these courses of study are valuable assets for the local churches, theologate faculty complain about the diffusion of their energies, leaving less time to focus on what has always been the primary mission of theologates—the formation of seminarians. Since some bishops are looking for institutions that are primarily devoted to seminarians, many schools have separated programs for lay students from seminarians. Discussion about the advisability of this division has supporters on both sides. Some believe that the interaction among seminarians and lay ecclesial students better prepares both groups for collaborating in ministry; others hold that seminarians need to solidify their identity as future priests and more fully embrace their vocation before engaging with the laity. Most bishops choose theologates where seminarians take courses separate from lay students.

Content of the Master of Divinity Curriculum

The requirements for the degree are based largely on the courses listed in the *PPF* as well as in interim directives such as the Apostolic Visitation of American seminaries report of 2008. For seminarians in the United States, these courses are usually organized around the MDiv degree. The average number of credits has increased from 107.7 in 1985–87 to 117.5 in 2013–15 (see appendix 6-A for credits required according to academic field).[3] While variations are found in how theologates name courses and assign credits, there is general correspondence to the directives of the *PPF.*

Overall, the number of credits has increased by ten, eight of which are in systematic theology, the only field that has experienced a significant increase. Scripture and systematic/dogmatic theology are two areas that are accorded the greatest importance. Pastoral studies and field education

---

[3] The averages by year are based on the most current catalog available in the given year, for example, for 2015, theologate catalogs used in compiling the averages ranged from 2013–15.

together also require a significant number of credits, reinforcing the notion that formation is to have a fundamentally pastoral character.[4]

Sacred Scripture

Understood as the "soul of all theology" and foundational to other studies, Sacred Scripture is given primary place in academic study and in daily meditation and liturgical celebrations. Reflecting the Vatican II document *Dei Verbum*, the fifth edition of the *PPF* treats the study of the Bible as essential to the intellectual formation of seminarians.[5] At least ten different areas are required as part of the core curriculum. In the Old Testament they are the Pentateuch, the historical, prophetic, and Wisdom books (especially the Psalms), and in the New Testament areas to be covered are the Synoptic Gospels and Acts, Pauline and Johannine literature, and the Catholic epistles (*PPF* V 199). Typically theologates actually require six courses: introduction to Bible/methodology of Old Testament/Old Testament introduction, prophets, Psalms and Wisdom literature, methodology of the New Testament/Synoptic Gospels, Pauline literature, and Johannine literature. To satisfy the requirements, some courses cover more than one of the prescribed areas. The average number of credit hours required in Scripture in 2015 was 17.8 (see appendix 6-B for details).[6]

There are some notable shifts in Scripture requirements from the first three editions of the *PPF* to the last two editions. In the first three, areas of study in Scripture are not specified. Instead, the authors offer general comments such as that the psalms are important for students' prayer life, that faculty should initiate students to biblical criticism so they under-

---

[4] On numerous occasions Pope Francis has spoken to seminarians about their preparation for priesthood in which he mentions all four pillars of formation, but he emphasizes the ultimate goal of preparation for priesthood as pastoral service, for example, in a talk presented to seminarians in Rome, on May 13, 2014, he said, "For leadership there is only one way: service. There is no other."

[5] See *Dei Verbum* (Dogmatic Constitution on Divine Revelation, 1965) 24; *PDV* 47, quoting St. Augustine's Sermon 179, says, "All clerics, particularly priests of Christ and others who, as deacons or catechists, are officially engaged in the ministry of the word, should immerse themselves in the Scriptures by constant sacred reading and diligent study. For it must not happen that anyone becomes 'an empty preacher of the word of God to others, not being a hearer of the word of God in his own heart.'"

[6] See commentary by Barbara Reid, "Trends in Scripture Study and Preaching Preparation in Roman Catholic Seminaries."

stand the message of the entire Scriptures, and that faculty should provide significant exercises in biblical criticism and exegesis of particular parts of the Scriptures. In contrast, the current edition states: "The proper understanding of Sacred Scripture requires the use of the historical-critical method, though this method is not totally sufficient. Other methods that are synchronic in approach are helpful in bringing forth the riches contained in the biblical texts" (*PPF* V 200, citing the Pontifical Biblical Commission's *The Interpretation of the Bible in the Church* [1993]). Recently, especially newer faculty tend to emphasize the latter and some of them question the use or value of the historical-critical method.

The fourth and fifth editions of the *PPF* are somewhat similar, naming many of the required courses identified above. The most notable changes called for in the fifth edition involved adding the Catholic epistles, which a few schools have done by combining them with Johannine literature, and dropping the requirements for introduction to the Old and New Testaments—which most theologates have not done. On the last point, the assumption of the authors of the *PPF* may have been that introductory Scripture courses are required in college seminary and pre-theology so students should have taken them before entering theology. However, experienced faculty have found that previous courses are of uneven quality and include introductory material in conjunction with teaching a particular book or books of the Bible. All agree that the study of Scripture and its interpretation should prepare seminarians for preaching and applying it to the lives of the faithful (*PPF* V 200). Scripture teachers, for example, are to help students do exegesis and other assignments with homilies in mind.

Systematic/Dogmatic Theology

The importance of systematic/dogmatic theology is second only to Sacred Scripture. In the first three editions of the *PPF*, the title for this area of the curriculum was "Systematic Theology and Sacred Liturgy." In the last two editions, the title was changed to "Dogmatic Theology and Sacramental/Liturgical Theology."[7] Seven topics in the early editions of

---

[7] Definitions of systematic theology usually include more areas of study than dogmatic theology. The prescribed courses in the last two editions of the *PPF* are broader in scope than the first three, so the less inclusive "dogmatic" nomenclature does not technically incorporate some of the areas, such as the sacramental/liturgical courses. The titles of this curricular area were changed without explanation. Remarks in *PDV*

the *PPF* defined the scope of systematic theology: Christology, ecclesiology, missiology, the Christian concept of God, and eschatology; for sacred liturgy there was required a general course on sacraments and liturgy and a separate course on Eucharist.[8] In sharp contrast, the last two editions of the *PPF* listed at least thirteen areas of study, though it is not possible to determine if all are to be separate courses. Dogmatic theology includes fundamental theology, ecclesiology, Christology, theology of God, One and Three (Trinity), creation, Fall, sin, redemption, grace, human person, eschatology, Mariology, missiology, and ecumenism. Sacramental/liturgical courses are to cover studies in the theological, historical, spiritual, pastoral, and juridical aspects of liturgy and sacraments, with particular attention to the sacrament of penance, Eucharist, and holy orders (which was listed as theology of priesthood with dogmatic theology in the fourth edition).

Explanation for the changes is limited to a comment about the new separate course on holy orders, which is to be "a thorough study of the nature and mission of the ministerial priesthood, including a history and theology of celibacy" (*PPF* V 202). The rationale for the extensive requirements provided in *PDV* is to prepare seminarians to be exemplary and capable teachers of the faith. Those who teach Christology and ecclesiology, for example, might ask students to consider how Christ is at work in parishes and how parishes function in relation to models of the church.

Because of its relationship to the believer, theology is led to pay particular attention both to the fundamental and permanent question of the relationship between faith and reason and to a number of requirements more closely related to the social and cultural situation of today. In regard to the first we have the study of fundamental theology, whose object is the fact of Christian revelation and its transmission in the church. In regard to the second we have disciplines that have been and are being developed as responses to problems strongly felt nowadays (*PDV* 54).

The specific courses and the rationale for the extensive requirements in this field are clear, but the response to them by theology faculty has been mixed. Virtually every curriculum complies by requiring the first set of dogmatic courses; however, only nine seminaries require ecumenism.

---

54 about this area of study are quite broad, commenting that the responsibility of communicating to others the Christian faith requires "the study of dogmatic and moral theology, of spiritual theology, of canon law and of pastoral theology."

  [8] After the first edition, apologetics was dropped as a requirement and only in the second edition were art, music, and communications mentioned.

The sacramental/liturgical requirements are generally followed.[9] Since many theologates have separate liturgy and/or sacramental departments, twelve more credits are required, over and above the credits for the nineteen systematic/dogmatic courses. Furthermore, spirituality courses are sometimes included in this area of the curriculum and amount to three credits. Studies in spirituality are to incorporate the Catholic spiritual tradition and the practical directives for the call to perfection and the capacity to offer to those entrusted to one's care (*PPF* V 212). Only nine schools require a course in spiritual direction, but all have at least one spirituality course. In some cases the apparent partial compliance relates to the way theologates categorize courses. Including courses in systematic/dogmatic theology, sacraments and liturgy, and spirituality, the average number of credit hours required in 2015 was 34.6 (see appendix 6-C for details).

Moral Theology

The attention given to moral theology and its placement in the curriculum has changed significantly as a result of Vatican II. The document that addresses the role of moral theology in seminary education is *OT*: "Special care is to be taken for the improvement of moral theology. Its scientific presentation, drawing more fully on the teaching of holy scripture, should highlight the lofty vocation of the Christian faithful and their obligation to bring forth fruit in charity for the life of the world" (16). Commenting on changes since this 1965 document, Jeremiah McCarthy writes that *OT* established the ecclesial blueprint for reform in priestly formation:

> The strengths of the Catholic tradition in moral theology have been rigor, clarity, and a commitment to the common good, anchored in a central conviction that our shared humanity provides us with the capacity to reach objective, moral truth. . . . New voices, including a diversity of perspectives, as well as an increased number of laymen and women scholars, have emerged in the Post-Vatican II era and they continue to enrich and deepen Catholic moral theology. The heightened awareness of the linkage between the spiritual and the moral life is a particularly fruitful and enduring legacy of the renewal called for by the Council for a more integrated, holistic moral theology

[9] Although only seventeen schools require holy orders, an additional fourteen require theology of priesthood as a dogmatic/systematic course, which satisfies the same requirement.

. . . This direction, hopefully, will continue in the ministry of future priests, "bearing fruit in charity for the life of the world."[10]

Although moral theology was one of the main branches of systematic theology before Vatican II, its importance has not always been highlighted, but this position gradually shifted. It is now treated as a distinct field of study in the *PPF.* The average number of credit hours required in moral theology in 2015 was 11.8 (see appendix 6-D for details). In the first *PPF*, the field was called "Moral and Ascetical Theology," and then, in the second and third editions, it became "Moral and Spiritual Theology." The description of the content did not include specific courses, but rather stated that the curriculum should embrace the theology and spirituality of the various states of Christian life, especially that of the priesthood. After publication of *PDV* in 1992, the last two *PPF*s separated out spiritual theology and listed four required courses under "moral theology": fundamental moral theology, medical-moral ethics, sexual morality, and social ethics. Extensive commentary on this area of study covers method and content. Moral theology "should be taught in a way that draws deeply from Sacred Scripture and Tradition, refers to the natural law and absolute moral norms, and gives consideration to the results of the natural and human sciences" and makes evident "the close link between moral, spiritual, and dogmatic theology" keeping clear "the pastoral task of priests as ministers of the Sacrament of Penance" (*PPF* V 205).[11] Special attention is to be given "to the fundamental respect for human life from conception to natural death and to the moral evils of and pastoral means of addressing contraception, abortion, and euthanasia" (*PPF* V 206). Responding to sexual abuse issues, *PPF* V states, "Adequate instruction must be given in professional ethics appropriate to priesthood and priestly ministry" (*PPF* V 209).

The guidelines of the *PPF* regarding the social teaching of the church require that it be presented in its entirety, including the social encyclicals.[12] The 2012 CARA report on "Justice and Equality: Formation in Catholic

---

[10] Reflection by Msgr. Jeremiah McCarthy, an experienced moral theology professor, seminary rector, past executive director of the NCEA Seminary Department, and a member of the advisory committee for this project, is currently moderator of the Curia, Diocese of Tucson.

[11] Here *PPF* V cites *Optatam Totius*, no. 16; *The Theological Formation of Future Priests*, 95–101; *Veritatis Splendor*, no. 95.

[12] See Congregation for Catholic Education, *Guidelines for the Study and Teaching of the Church's Social Doctrine in the Formation of Priests* (1988).

Social Teaching and Intercultural Competency in Seminary Programs" provided a thorough analysis of how social teaching is regarded in seminaries.[13] Nearly all (95 percent) of the rectors/presidents responded to the survey and on the whole gave a favorable accounting of the way Catholic social teaching (CST) is integrated into the curriculum. They agreed that it is "very well integrated into moral theology classes, pastoral ministry classes, and pastoral placements of seminarians." They are less positive "in their evaluation of how well CST is integrated into scripture, preaching, spirituality, and liturgy classes." Likewise, results showed that some themes are covered more effectively than others—the defense of human life from conception to natural death, the scriptural foundations for defending life and dignity, the defense of marriage, and the promotion of family life. Other themes are not as effectively communicated, such as human rights, the common good, and priority for the poor and vulnerable. The survey did not inquire about whether students participated in activities related to social justice issues; however, in interviews with faculty, most reported that compared to ten or more years ago, relatively few students initiate or engage in projects such as volunteering in soup kitchens, helping with collection and distribution of clothing and food for the poor, and similar activities.

Historical Studies

Appreciation for the study of history, if it is to be judged by the number of courses required in *PPF* V, has diminished and shifted in focus. The first four editions required six similar areas of study: early church history and patristics, medieval, modern, and contemporary history, and American church history. The most recent *PPF* lists only three: patrology and patristics, history of the church universal, and history of the Catholic Church in the United States, which is to reflect its multicultural origins and ecumenical context. It specifies, "Among historical studies, the study of patristics and the lives of the saints are of special importance" (*PPF* V 210). Ironically, theologates have not responded entirely to the directives; while only three courses rather than six are now required according to the *PPF*, most theologates require four to cover the areas of patristics, the early/medieval periods, modern/contemporary periods, and American Catholic Church history. The average number of credit hours required in

---

[13] Mary L. Gautier and C. Joseph O'Hara, A Report to the Secretariat of Clergy, Consecrated Life and Vocations of the USCCB (2012), 2–3.

historical studies was up slightly from 8.6 credits in 1987 to 9.8 in 2015 (see appendix 6-E for details).

Pastoral Theology

This area, which until the current *PPF* was called pastoral studies, is a complex and essential dimension of seminary formation. The many recent adjustments in requirements are related to parish structures, the necessities of parish life, and the limited experience of seminarians relative to parish processes and procedures. Although *PDV* incorporates all of these areas of study under one heading, most theologates separate the fields according to the norms of the *PPF*. It encompasses four disciplines: pastoral theology/skills, homiletics, canon law, and liturgical practica, which according to *PPF* V should incorporate twelve areas of study. Until *PPF* V, eight areas were prescribed, giving only minimal details about the offerings. On average, theologates now require twenty-four credit hours in ten courses, not all of which match exactly the *PPF*. They are divided roughly as follows: eight credits in pastoral theology/skills, six in homiletics, five in canon law, and five in liturgical practica (see appendix 6-F for details).

In *pastoral theology/skills* courses, two areas have similar content, but have undergone several iterations. First, Christian education has become evangelization and catechesis. Although priests engage in a considerable amount of teaching in parishes, sometimes in a regular classroom, methods or approaches to teaching are not required by the *PPF*. Nonetheless, half of the theologates do require such a course, all but one of them diocesan. Pastoral guidance has evolved to pastoral counseling with widely varying course descriptions. The content focuses on general principles, marriage and family, or counseling for confession. Two other early requirements, sociology of religion and ascetics, have been dropped in favor of pastoral theology and marriage and the family. The latter is sometimes listed as part of the counseling course or under sacraments as a marriage course.

Homiletics, the second area, termed "preaching" in the first *PPF* and then simply "skills in pedagogy, psychology, and communication," now receives lengthy treatment. This change responds both to the often registered disappointment of Catholics with homilies and to the attention given the topic by church leaders. In recent years, every pope has stressed the importance of preaching, and USCCB documents have emphasized the necessity of sound preaching if evangelization is to be successful. A series of seventeen USCCB editions of *Fulfilled in Your Hearing: The Homily in the Sunday Assembly,* from 1982 to 2002, was followed by *Preaching the Mystery of Faith: The Sunday Homily* (2012).[14]

Besides these documents, the 2013 apostolic exhortation *Evangelii Gaudium* by Pope Francis includes an expansive exposition on preparing for and delivering a homily (chap. 3). He says it must be inculturated, be spoken from the heart, deal with beauty and goodness, set people on fire with love of the Lord, and be carefully prepared, since it "is so important a task that a prolonged time of study, prayer, reflection and pastoral creativity should be devoted to it" (EG 145). This sort of enthusiastic endorsement has led to greater attention to the teaching of preaching:

> Homiletics should occupy a prominent place in the core curriculum and be integrated into the entire course of studies. In addition to the principles of biblical interpretation, catechesis, and communications theory, seminarians should also learn the practical skills needed to communicate the Gospel as proclaimed by the Church in an effective and appropriate manner. (*PPF* V 215)

At the same time faculty understand how difficult it is to prepare inspiring preachers. Generally, seminarians have inadequate background in public speaking and are not as familiar with the culture as they should be if homilies are to resonate with parishioners. Moreover, in many theologates, those teaching homiletics are adjunct professors, often excellent preachers, but not often trained in how to teach others to preach.

In the third area, requirements in *canon law* were specified in detail only in the last two editions of the *PPF*. The two courses are "Introduction to Canon Law" and "Canon Law of Individual Sacraments," including the sacrament of matrimony. Previously, only a general requirement in canon law was mentioned, but *PPF* V references the 1983 Code of Canon Law ninety-one times, giving an indication of its guiding force in the entire *PPF*. In the fourth area linked to pastoral theology, two topics were added to *liturgical practica*, one for the sacrament of penance and the other for the Eucharist and sacraments in general; also, directives were given for

---

[14] Illustrating why homilies are so important, the bishops listed reasons why Catholics seem "indifferent to or disaffected with the Church and her teaching," besides the fact that "many Catholics, even those who are devoted to the life of the Church and hunger for a deeper spirituality, seem to be uninformed about the Church's teaching and are in need of a stronger catechesis" (USCCB, *Preaching the Mystery of Faith: The Sunday Homily* [2012] 5).

music, art, and architecture. The additions and specifications in pastoral theology generally resulted in more requirements and a shift in priorities. Overall since 1987, the changes may seem minimal in the aggregate, but they are substantial in emphasis.

B. Pastoral Formation

This area covers what is commonly known as field education or supervised pastoral ministry. It has taken on greater meaning in recent years as entering seminarians lack broad parish experience and familiarity with church ministry in general. The experience requires students to observe and perform ministry under the supervision of priests and other professionals in various areas. Although the number of credits has dropped slightly from twelve to ten between 1987 and 2015, seminarians spend more time in ministry settings, especially in summers, when they do not necessarily receive academic credit. A wide variety of time frames and settings are employed by theologates, and theological reflection and evaluation are expected dimensions of a field placement as made clear in *PPF* V:

> Supervision, theological reflection, and evaluation are necessary components of an effective pastoral program. Although theological reflection can help the development of pastoral skills, its primary purpose is to interpret pastoral experience or activity in light of Scripture, church teaching, personal faith, and pastoral practices. Reflection of this kind should become a lifelong habit in priestly ministry. (248)

As for *time spent in a field placement*, some schools require a semester or even a complete academic year in full-time supervised ministry, while others use summers, and a few utilize continuous parish placement over all four years of theology. The latter, called a "teaching parish program," usually has a particular emphasis each semester, for example, the mission of a parish, pastoral care, youth faith formation, RCIA and adult formation, ministerial relationships, and leadership and administration. With each succeeding semester, students take on more responsibility with the guidance of a supervisor and parish committee, which is comprised of older and younger, married and single members. Students are exposed to all the typical ministries of a parish, such as liturgical leadership, several levels of education, nursing home and hospital visitations, fundraising, communications, and others.[15]

---

[15] This format has been in effect at the Saint Paul Seminary School of Divinity since 1983. Similar programs are now being implemented in several other theologates.

Other time frames usually involve being present full time in a parish or other ministry setting with participation in all activities for a semester or shorter time. One advantage of the teaching parish is being able to experience in greater depth the seasons in the life of a parish, but its shortcoming is the limited exposure to different types of parishes. Full-time shorter placements provide greater variety, but with a less comprehensive view of the parish. A *pastoral year* is required by seven theologates, usually after second theology, and typically has the seminarian returning to his home diocese or religious community to engage in a full-time supervised program. Eight theologates sponsor a pastoral year that is optional, and it is always available to a seminarian at the request of his diocese, but it may not always be supervised by the school.

Summer placements are often used for specialized ministry in a variety of parish settings, such as a very large parish, multiple parishes under one pastor, or a predominately ethnic parish.[16] Other ministerial settings also are used, more often for seminarians who belong to religious orders. They may be involved in such areas as teaching and educational leadership, campus ministry or other chaplaincies, retreat ministry, and justice advocacy. Until recently, Clinical Pastoral Education (CPE), an interfaith professional program to teach pastoral care in health care settings, was required by almost all theologates. The ten-week summer placement was considered an important venue for an ecumenical experience that brought together in a supervised encounter students of all faiths as they worked with patients of diverse religious backgrounds. Currently, only nine schools require CPE, and seven others offer it as an option. Replacing the official CPE program, some schools provide the option of a short hospital ministry unit, but usually lacking the ecumenical encounter and not always with trained supervisors.

---

[16] Several theologates provide placements in Hispanic parishes and in the school maintain a supportive environment for incorporating practices that are predominant among Hispanic Catholics. They feature courses in other disciplines in which they use Spanish as the language of instruction, especially in homiletics and liturgical practica. Integrating an understanding of the faith from other than the North American perspective should be the goal of every discipline, given the changing demographics of the church in the United States. According to *PDV* 55, "In the face of all the different and at times contrasting cultures present in the various parts of the world, inculturation seeks to obey Christ's command to preach the Gospel to all nations even unto the ends of the earth." It reinforces the demand for the evangelization of cultures and the inculturation of the message of faith, but few faculty have the background or experience to fully implement this approach.

Those who were directors of pastoral formation in 2015 came from significantly different backgrounds than those who served prior to 2005. According to *PPF* V, the director of pastoral formation has to be a priest if the position requires more than organizing various field experiences (340). Consequently, directors are increasingly diocesan and religious priests, a shift from 45 percent to 69 percent since 2005. Others who were not clergy serving as directors of pastoral formation have decreased as a result of this shift. At present, especially the larger theologates list women as associate or assistant directors, many of whom report that they continue to manage the same duties as they did when they were directors. Fifty percent of those serving as directors of pastoral formation hold doctorates, compared with 33 percent in 1997 and 42 percent in 1987. The improved percentage of doctoral degrees may be due to those who hold dual positions in teaching or administration that require a doctorate. Those with faculty rank have moved from 35 percent in 1987 to 72 percent in 2015.

Overall pastoral experiences are highly valued by bishops who, in many cases, will be assigning recently ordained men as pastors, sometimes of more than one parish. The content and intensity of their field experiences vary according to the regard in which pastoral formation is held by the faculty. A higher proportion than ever of faculty are not priests or religious, many of whom have no pastoral experience, and often they are not able to provide a pastoral perspective in their courses. Some of them believe that priests should learn on the job, and they voice the opinion that pastoral formation detracts from academic studies.

The struggle to achieve the proper allotment of time for each area of formation is ongoing. No single formula is used by all theologates. The unanswered question is how well newly ordained priests and their lay ecclesial ministry colleagues are able to serve the people of God in parish and other ministerial assignments. The test of any curriculum needs to be measured against this standard. Otherwise, what appears theoretically well-balanced and coherent has limited resonance with a rapidly changing Catholic population in an equally rapidly changing culture.

PART IV

Conclusion and Commentaries

Chapter 7

New Directions in the Future

How well are seminaries and theologates preparing graduates for ministry in the church? The research in this book, covering the past thirty years, reveals changes that can seem inconsequential year to year, but when viewed over a long span of time are remarkable in their magnitude. Church ministry and ultimately the lives of the Catholic faithful will be significantly affected by the way priests and laypeople are prepared to serve. How the church prepares them always needs to be an urgent concern.[1]

More than thirty years ago when I began studying seminaries, the results were published in the book *Reason for the Hope: The Futures of Roman Catholic Theologates*. At the time, the reference to hope resonated with many, and I was often asked what my reasons were for being hopeful. In those years of the mid-1980s, seminary and theologate leaders had embraced the teachings of the Second Vatican Council and were implementing programs in response to the directions set out in *OT* and other council documents related to theological education. As I set about writing this book, the same question about hope remains. As a person of faith, my answer is certainly in the affirmative although there are issues and challenges that require constant reflection and purposeful action.

As described in the preceding chapters and the commentaries that follow, many positive developments have been instituted in recent years. *PDV* launched human formation programs that took seriously the deep personal

---

[1] See commentary by Msgr. Peter Vaccari, "The Culture of Encounter: The Future of Seminary Formation."

development of those who would be ministerial leaders. In addition, it became unequivocally clear that the goal of all formation must be pastoral in nature. Admissions standards were reviewed and strengthened. Accreditation by the ATS brought virtually all Catholic theologates into dialogue with a wider range of seminaries. Especially in recent years, collaboration between the NCEA Seminary Department and the USCCB Committee on Clergy, Consecrated Life and Vocations resulted in significant publications and programs that were invaluable resources to theologates and in the research for this book. Individual accomplishments by theologates and their administrators and faculty were outstanding. Theologates made great strides in programming for a growing multicultural student population, including more international students. In some theologates, strong lay student enrollment resulted in high-quality programs and innovation in lay formation for ministry. In general, schools are now in a more stable financial position, thanks in great part to expanded institutional advancement programs and to a recovering economy.

My hope for the future rests on the theologates making improvements in directions that respond more fully to the spiritual needs in people's lives and the requirements of the new evangelization. As I reflect on my research, certain specific recommendations emerge that I suggest are evident in the data. While it is the responsibility of researchers to report faithfully their findings, we also have an obligation to raise up for wider consideration what these findings seem to suggest. I begin with three broad recommendations and then move to some practical aspects of the formation process that merit attention.

1. All programs need to be reviewed in light of greater knowledge of the church as it exists presently in the United States, especially in its multicultural dimensions, and in light of a deeper understanding of secular culture, particularly of young people, in order to reach and inspire today's Catholics.

2. An honest appraisal must be made of what seems to have alienated so many Catholics from the faith of their birth, especially those of the millennial generation. Is it the qualities of ministry or of those who minister? This requires theologates to resist the temptation to be self-justifying or self-protective as they consider how they are forming students to respond. As a side note, one of the most frequently mentioned issues in my research and in the research of others is the importance of finding a resolution of differences in perception and implementation of ministry between senior pastors/priests and young/newly ordained priests.

3. Future priests and lay ministers must be taught the knowledge, skills, and attitudes essential for authentic collaboration and mutual appreciation. Guided by the attitudes and directives laid out in *Co-Workers in the Vineyard of the Lord*, faculty will need to make concerted efforts to change patterns of separation and competition that seem to contradict the vision of the bishops. *Co-Workers* notes, for instance, "An ecclesiology of communion looks upon different gifts and functions not as adversarial but as enriching and complementary."[2]

Other recommendations to keep hope alive are narrower in scope and more particular to specific areas of formation. Individual institutions will find some suggestions more applicable than others, but each of them represents common concerns.

1. Readiness for theology-level studies in the present cultural and ecclesial circumstances requires a review of the prescribed curricula of both college and pre-theology programs. Courses that provide an understanding of the human person and of society, as prescribed in *PDV*,[3] should be included as well as courses in communications and public speaking.

2. Identifying pastoral implications should be required in every course so that seminarians and lay ministry students come to understand the treasures of the faith not as abstract ideals but as living, practical principles integral to faithful Christian living.

3. Faculty need initial and ongoing education and formation themselves about topics that have not been part of their specialized academic backgrounds. In particular, those who are not familiar with all aspects of formation should be apprised of how to work more effectively with both seminarians and lay students.

---

[2] USCCB, *Co-Workers in the Vineyard of the Lord: A Resource for Guiding the Development of Lay Ecclesial Ministry* (Washington, DC: USCCB, 2005), 20. The quote continues: "It appreciates the Church's unity as an expression of the mutual and reciprocal gifts brought into harmony by the Holy Spirit. An ecclesiology of communion recognizes diversity in unity and acknowledges the Spirit as the source of all the gifts that serve to build up Christ's Body (1 Cor 12:4-12, 28-30). For 'to each is given the manifestation of the Spirit for the common good'" (1 Cor 12:7).

[3] *PDV* 52 states, "For a deeper understanding of man and the phenomena and lines of development of society, in relation to a pastoral ministry which is as 'incarnate' as possible, the so-called 'human sciences' can be of considerable use, sciences such as sociology, psychology, education, economics and politics, and the science of social communication."

4. In general, all those who share in the responsibility for seminary formation, from boards of trustees to administration and faculty, would benefit from interaction with peers in other institutions. This type of mutual ongoing education and reflection might be achieved through regular meetings and conferences as well as in-house workshops and retreats.

5. Special attention to maintaining admissions standards, especially in the face of insufficient numbers of seminarians, is essential. Admission of all students should take into account the personal and professional qualities needed for effective ministry. Assessment should be thorough and honest, always keeping in mind the good of the church and the increasingly rigorous demands on pastoral leaders in a complex, pluralistic, and skeptical world.

Even with the data available in this study and other research reports, the ultimate questions about the effectiveness of ministerial education are incomplete. Questions we must continue to pursue include:

- How do those receiving the ministry of recent seminary graduates—priests and lay ministers—experience their services?

- How effective are bishops, pastors, and coworkers in aligning their desire to collaborate with actual practice?

- How can the church help bridge the divide between many new clergy and their senior colleagues?

- What are the steps needed to capitalize on the gifts of the ordained and lay ecclesial ministers in order to advance mutual respect and common effort?

In answer to those questions, a great deal of information is available about a few parishes and other institutions, anecdotes are abundant, and opinions are endless, but widespread research has not been undertaken. A detailed and extensive survey of bishops, religious superiors, pastors working with the newly ordained and new lay ecclesial ministers, and parishioners would provide powerful insights about the ministry and those who are providing it. Until we have more information that measures accomplishments and dissatisfactions, it is impossible to provide a definitive answer to the question I most often receive: "What makes a seminary or school of theology an excellent place to prepare for ministry?" Though that question continues to draw forward all of us concerned about the mission of the church, this book represents my effort to report plainly and honestly what can be discerned now from the available information about the seminaries and theologates serving the church in the United States.

Excellence in ministerial formation will continue to be a concern for generations to come. Inspiration to stay steady to the task and to cultivate hope lies beyond the "perfect program." Pope Francis, speaking at World Mission Day in 2013, raised up a vision that might set a standard for all formation:

> The men and women of our time need the secure light that illuminates their path and that only the encounter with Christ can give. Let us bring to the world, through our witness, with love, the hope given by faith! The Church's missionary spirit is not about proselytizing, but the testimony of a life that illuminates the path, which brings hope and love. The Church—I repeat once again—is not a relief organization, an enterprise or an NGO, but a community of people, animated by the Holy Spirit, who have lived and are living the wonder of the encounter with Jesus Christ and want to share this experience of deep joy, the message of salvation that the Lord gave us. It is the Holy Spirit who guides the Church in this path. (4)

In the end, this is the noble purpose that challenges seminarians and laypeople alike as they present themselves as candidates for service as pastoral leaders. Theologates must equip them with the knowledge, skills, personal insight, and spiritual fervor needed to enable people to encounter Christ. And while formation requires human enterprise and ingenuity, Pope Francis reminds us that its ultimate source rests in God "who guides the Church in this path."

Therein lies my hope and, I believe, the hope of all those concerned about formation for ministry.

> They that hope in the LORD will renew their strength,
>   they will soar on eagles' wings;
> They will run and not grow weary,
>   walk and not grow faint. (Isa 40:31)

Toward a Spirituality
of Ecclesial Leadership

Ronald Rolheiser, OMI
President, Oblate School of Theology
San Antonio, Texas

The first task in leadership is to radiate life and inspire others.

Defining the Task

What should we, ideally, look for in an ordained priest?

At one level, the answer is clear: We are looking for someone who can effectively instruct, heal, and draw others into community around the person of Jesus Christ and who can sustain himself in spiritual, moral, and psychological integrity throughout his ministry so as to incarnate what he teaches and radiate the life and joy of the Gospel.

But there are a variety of understandings of what that might look like concretely and how we should educate a seminarian to get there. Differing views of the church, differing concepts of ministry, and differing understandings of priesthood offer diverse pictures of what this might look like and what the process of formation should be. In any clergy gathering today, there will be priests who draw their concepts of priesthood and ministry primarily out of the vision of Vatican II and, by contrast, priests who have negative reactions to precisely those concepts of ministry and priesthood. Sometimes this is named as the difference between being a "Vatican II priest" as opposed to a "John Paul II priest." However careless and oversimplified that distinction, one sees that the ideal of Roman

122

Catholic priesthood can be carried in different ways—and, indeed, has been carried in very different ways throughout the history of the church.

Hence, seminary formation must deal more reflectively and deliberately with the questions: What should an ideal priest look like? What ecclesiology should he radiate? What should be the key qualities and attitudes that he brings to ministry? How should seminary formation augment his natural aptitudes, sincerity, piety, and goodwill? What are nonnegotiable aspects within seminary formation? Finally, how should the "signs of the times" affect how we form candidates for ordination?

The intent of this commentary is to try to *name* the key elements that seminaries should be emphasizing as they seek to form men as priests. These reflections are, admittedly, influenced and colored by what I see personally as emphasized and underemphasized in Roman Catholic seminaries today. I submit that, beyond the many good things we are already doing, we need to put special emphasis on seven elements: *training for leadership, solid academics, spirituality, wide catholicity, reading the signs of the times, commitment to the poor,* and *servant-leadership.*

Elements of the Task

1. Forming the Candidate for Leadership

While the priesthood is a vocation, not a profession, it nonetheless demands that one be a professional within that vocation. In forming seminarians for the priesthood, we may never forget that we are forming them to lead Christian communities, at times very large ones and almost always complex. The task of forming seminarians to be leaders may never be bracketed simply because a candidate is a sincere, pious, and prayerful man. These are admirable qualities, but alone they are not enough for ordination. A priest needs to be capable of significant leadership.

A model drawn from the medical profession might be helpful here. In the area of medicine, there are various levels of service. Some people are capable of providing simple first aid, some drive an ambulance, some have special training as first responders, others act as nurse aids, others are fully registered nurses, and some are doctors who function as general practitioners or are specialists in various areas of medicine. If one applies this kind of paradigm to Roman Catholic ministries, one sees that an ordained priest (unless he is sent for further specialized studies) is meant to serve like a doctor at the level of a general practitioner. He need not be a specialist (like any doctor he can refer what is beyond his competence to various specialists), but he needs to be able to function as a basic "doctor" of the soul. This demands that he be more than a capable dispenser of the sacraments.

Beyond the spiritual and pastoral skills demanded of them as leaders, most Roman Catholic priests will find themselves quite soon after ordination, in effect, the CEO of a parish community and often a large physical plant. Obviously, we need not train our seminarians to be full professional administrators, but we must train them to be wise enough leaders to know how to properly delegate those administrative tasks of which they are incapable of fulfilling either because of time or competence. Again, sincerity and piety alone are not equal to this task. We must ensure that we form seminarians for leadership.

2. Providing Candidates with Solid Academic Training

Closely tied to forming candidates for leadership is the need to ensure that they receive solid academic and theological training. Serious and critical study of theology may not be bypassed in favor of catechesis, an overview of church doctrine, or a general understanding of canon law. A seminarian needs to be prepared to face the hard and demanding questions he will meet as a priest ministering in a world where people are far less docile than previous generations.

To offer just one type of example of what is at issue here: as the president of a theological school that teaches seminarians, I have had many conversations through the years with various bishops, vocation directors, and seminary formators regarding the extent to which the academic theology that is being taught in our classrooms should challenge the seminarians on their piety, their often naïve and uncritical theology, their defensiveness toward other Christians and other faiths, and their desire to shield themselves from hearing the type of criticism being made of the church by various secular thinkers, including many feminist authors. Almost invariably, the concern of bishops, vocation directors, and seminary formation directors is that we do not push the seminarians too strongly in terms of the strong criticisms being leveled at the church. That concern has its own legitimacy. It recognizes that many of our seminarians today are, in a word, fragile, at least insofar as their faith is concerned. Their faith is often young, is surrounded by threat, and many times lacks a proper catechetical foundation (let alone a proper theological foundation). They are, indeed, young seedling plants needing protection from the harsher elements of the weather before they are ready.

In fact, the etymology of the word "seminary," that is, *seminarium*, means a greenhouse that protects and nurtures young plants. While seminarians must indeed receive special nurturing, they must also be given the resources to eventually survive in the wild. Hence, seminaries must walk a delicate line between overexposing and underexposing seminarians to the harshest elements of criticism within the present-day intellectual and ecclesial climate. The youth and fervor of their faith and their fearfulness must be respected, even as we recognize that if we overprotect them during their seminary years, there is a good chance they will overprotect themselves afterwards. This may take the form of listening and ministering to only their own kind and to those who do not threaten them. Overprotection also risks producing a priest who at some point might go to the other extreme and look back on his own formation with bitterness, as was the case so commonly with priests and religious who, after Vatican II, bitterly rejected the oversheltered formation they had received in seminaries and convents.

Linked to this is the importance of including study of the arts and human sciences in a seminarian's formation. My personal anxiety is that this is not being sufficiently valued today. For example, during the 2008 Apostolic Visitation of seminaries, the concern of the visitation team seemed to lock in primarily around the question of orthodoxy within dogmatic and moral theology and a fear of feminism. Are our seminarians orthodox and loyal? Is there undue feminist influence in our seminaries? Nowhere, it seems, was there a concern expressed as to whether the seminarian was open to the world, to laity, to women, and to the arts. I doubt any seminarian was asked any of these questions: "What is the last novel you read?" "When did you last go to an opera?" "Have you read any books of social criticism recently?" Or even: "Do you watch the world news every day?"

Hard, critical academics and theology need to be nonnegotiable within a seminarian's training, as indeed the *PPF* mandates. Every time the church has cheated on this and decided that a good heart and piety were enough for priestly ordination, it has paid a price. It is no accident that the first thing Roman Catholicism did in response to the Reformation was to institute a new academic rigor into seminary training.

3. Ensuring That the Candidate Develops a Sustaining Spirituality

A priest is meant to be a spiritual-wisdom figure, an elder, one who can help guide peoples' souls, both through his preaching and in one-to-one pastoral situations. Hence an important emphasis in his training must be on spirituality: how to nurture a soul, how to guide a soul, how to teach people how to pray, and how to read the movements of the soul. He need not be a specialist in this, but he needs to be at the level of a general practitioner as a spiritual doctor. The classic negative example of this is the fact that today most priests do not know how to give one-to-one spiritual direction and are very insecure in guiding anyone's prayer life. This is a fault in our present seminary formation.

There is a second component to this as well: seminary formation must try to develop within its candidates a personal spirituality that is strong enough to sustain the candidate through the ups and downs of a long marathon journey in ministry with its perennial temptations toward inflation or depression. When I think back on my own seminary formation, I see that it was strong in teaching me how to do ministry, but it was weak in preparing me *for what ministry would be doing to me*, that is: What would be my temptations to depression, inflation, compensatory actions, manipulation of others, escapism, and anger as I fulfilled my pastoral calling? Seminary formation must strive to develop inside seminarians a personal spirituality that will give them sufficient bread for the long haul. These interior resources are not just for surviving in the priesthood but for finding joy there and for being a minister of joy to others.

It goes without saying, seminary formation must give special attention to helping prepare seminarians to live out their celibacy in a way that makes it a joyful gift to others and not something that leaves them, in whatever way, neutered, bitter, unable to deal with sexual complexity, and prone to compensatory behavior. Admittedly, this is not an easy task, but it is a critical one.

4. Forming Our Candidates for a Wide Catholicity

The opposite of "Catholic" is not "Protestant." The opposite of "Catholic" is narrow, small-minded, small-hearted, elitist, and exclusive. The word "catholic" means universal, wide, inclusive, and all-embracing. Perhaps the best definition of the word is given by Jesus when, in the gospels, he says, "In my Father's house there are many rooms." In saying this, Jesus was not talking about architecture in heaven but about the width and depth of God's heart. God's heart is not a ghetto, a single room, a single ideology, or a single ethnicity, religion, or gender. God's love embraces everyone without discrimination. As Jesus so stunningly says, *God lets his sun shine on the good as well as the bad.* God's love is nondiscriminatory;

it is "catholic" in the real sense of that word. As well, both testaments in our Scriptures make it clear that God is a "jealous" God, that is, a God who is anxious to have everyone come to the table, not just those of one's own kind. The Good Shepherd seeks relentlessly and lovingly after "those other sheep who are not of this flock."

Seminarians must be trained to radiate this kind of universality and inclusivity. Very practically, this means challenging them more strongly and teaching them to be more sensitive to ecumenism and interfaith dialogue and cooperation. Too often today, these sensitivities are seen as optional to the priest's ministry. Ecumenism and interfaith outreach are central to our catholicity and not a matter of choosing to be involved depending upon one's time, temperament, and energy.

I highlight this because I fear indifference to ecumenism and interfaith outreach might be more the norm than the exception. At the school where I teach, we host an evening of prayer for church unity each January during the Week of Prayer for Christian Unity. We have more than one hundred diocesan and religious seminarians studying at our school and normally not a single seminarian shows up for this ecumenical event. It is not that these seminarians are anti-ecumenical; it is rather that the whole issue of other churches and other religions is simply not on their radar screens. We must do a better job of sensitizing seminarians in this area.

The same holds true for working with laity and working with women. We must try to instill a wider catholicity here. Seminarians need to form a clerical identity, but in fostering this, we must be vigilant against fostering clericalism at the same time. Indeed, Pope Francis has been issuing clear and repeated warnings about this topic.

5. *Forming Candidates to Read the Signs of the Times*

While much of seminarian formation needs to be the same for every age and is not particularly subject to the changing times, there are aspects within it that are "signs of the times" to which each generation must respond creatively and pastorally. Given today's cultural, intellectual, and ecclesial climate, at least in North America and Western Europe, what are some "signs" that seminaries need to read and address more explicitly inside their formation programs? I venture to name two such interrelated signs:

   a. Today, certainly in North America and Western Europe, there is an intellectual bias, stemming back to the Enlightenment, against

Christianity and this has helped spawn among other things a strong anticlericalism. In certain places where, for centuries, the priest could not say anything wrong, today he cannot say anything right. The public perception of a priest has moved from a former position of privilege to a present position of dis-privilege.

b. Formerly a priest was ordained into an assured status and respect. The office of priesthood used to more or less automatically confer a certain respect and credibility on a person. Today, given the anti-clericalism within the culture and the impact of the sexual abuse crisis, the opposite is more often true. The man being ordained has to give credibility to the office and show that he and it are worthy of respect.

Seminaries must form seminarians in light of this. A priest today who still blissfully believes that the office of priesthood will, of itself, accord him credibility and respect and who, worse still, looks for clerical privilege will not bring credibility and respect to the church, nor will he provide an effective ministry. As well, for those who are aware of this anticlerical bias in the culture, the task is to teach them not to "over-read" this concern, not to take it personally, and especially not to become defensive and have a "martyr complex" in the face of it. The priest's task is rather to earn respect and credibility for the church, the priesthood, and himself. And he must accept this task joyfully, without self-pity, and without an unhealthy nostalgia about how things used to be.

The issue of clerical dress and religious habits impact upon this. When to wear them and when not to wear them? Today, most times we are witnessing the two extremes vis-à-vis clerical attire: that wearing a Roman collar or religious habit is an integral part of the priesthood and a *sine qua non* for being a good priest or that clerical attire should be completely abandoned. Both of these are unhappy positions and both more invested in an ecclesial ideology than in a genuine desire to truly put one's gifts at the service of the world and the church. The issue of clerical dress and religious habits is a practical one, not a theological one, and it needs to be more explicitly and reflectively addressed within seminary formation, particularly given the anti-Christian and anticlerical bias within the culture heightened by the sexual abuse crisis.

6. Forming Candidates to Serve the Poor

No one gets to heaven without a letter of reference from the poor, least of all a minister of the Gospel. Perhaps the best criterion by which to judge authentic Christian discipleship in our world is to look at who is moving downwards. Who fits the description given by St. Paul in the Letter to Philippians (2:6-7) when he says of Jesus, "Though he was in the form of God, / [Jesus] did not regard equality with God something to be grasped. / Rather, he emptied himself, / taking the form of a slave"? When this is applied to priesthood and ministry, a priest should be moving downward.

To be ordained a priest is to be privileged—an envied education, a sacred ministry, access to huge worldwide resources, personal financial security, well-funded health care, and an important place within community. These are major gifts, richer than what is given to the vast majority of people in our world. The priest need not apologize about this. Indeed God would like for everyone to have these gifts. But, as the Philippians hymn makes clear, these gifts are not something to be grasped at. Rather, like Jesus, the priest must constantly be emptying himself by, among other things, immersing himself in the lives of the poor and letting his gifts bless them, even as he receives a rich blessing from them in return. The priest must model what it means to be a true disciple of Jesus: stepping downward into a second baptism—immersion into the poor—where community and joy are found.

The poor have many faces, and normally they will present themselves so the priest need not go look for them. But sometimes, especially in some of our more affluent parishes and ministry settings, the poor who present themselves are not the economically poor, that is, those who (as Gustavo Gutiérrez defines the poor) "do not have the right to have rights." How does a priest, in that kind of setting, immerse himself in the lives of the poor? He does it by being especially attentive to the classical "corporal works of mercy" and assuring that in some way he is ministering to those who do not have the "right to have rights."

During the past half-century, seminaries have been quite sensitive to the area of social justice and have healthily challenged seminarians in that area. That emphasis needs to continue since, as Jesus assures us, the poor we will always have with us and there is a privileged presence of God within them.

7. Forming Candidates for Servant Leadership

Jesus defined his own leadership style in these words: "I have come to serve, not to be served" (see Matt 20:28). He also says of his followers (even though they walk *behind* him in discipleship), "I have called you friends" (John 15:15). Finally, and perhaps most significantly as an indicator of his ethos of leadership, Jesus washes his disciples' feet, giving us "a model to follow" (John 13:15).

What Jesus modeled for us is commonly termed *servant leadership*, and it was a scandal to the people of his generation and remains a scandal to people of our own generation. Superiors are not supposed to wash the feet of subordinates. Important leaders are not supposed to do menial tasks for their employees. CEOs are not supposed to serve coffee at the board meeting. Faculty members are not supposed to be helping the janitor mop the floors. And popes, bishops, and priests are not supposed to let others tell them how to run the church. Servant leadership, as modeled by Jesus, is still a rare thing, both in civil and church circles.

The priesthood is a vocation to serve, and in forming candidates for it we must constantly emphasize that this is not a position of power, status, privilege, specialness, and separateness from others. While we need to help our candidates find a healthy clerical identity, it must not be based on emphasizing separation, privilege, or status. All of these go directly against what Jesus modeled for us as servant leadership. Very practically today, this means a willingness to be more open to listen to people, to share decision making, to (in the words of Pope Francis) take on the "smell of the sheep," and, perhaps most importantly of all, to be less guarded in letting ourselves be loved and "ordained" by the people we serve.

The concept of servant leadership pertains as well to clerical celibacy since it contains within itself a special element of self-renunciation. However, for a priest, what is given up in the vow or promise of celibacy is not, first of all, meant to be a renunciation *per se*. Rather, commitment to celibacy is meant precisely to make the priest available so that he can embrace everyone and make family with everyone. Indeed, that is why he is called "father." He is a member of every family. While sleeping with no one and having no human family or children of his own, his sexuality and paternity, in a very real way, reach out to make family of everyone.

Forming seminarians for servant leadership, however, is contingent upon a certain image of the church. If one thinks of the church as a castle to be defended or a treasure chest of truths to be protected, then ministry will more naturally be seen more as a military function (guarding the gates of truth) than as servant leadership. If, however, the church is seen more, as Pope Francis suggests, as a "field hospital" that is attending to the wounded, the concept of ministry as servant leadership flows more naturally. Seminary formation must be quite deliberate in undergirding its concepts of ministry (and these are plural) on various concepts of the church (and these are also plural). However, the concept of servant leadership must undergird all the other concepts of ministry.

Given the death of clerical privilege within secularized culture, given the need for a more radical witness in the wake of the sexual abuse crisis, and, more importantly, given the example of Jesus, everything inside our seminary formation must emphasize servant leadership, non-privilege, and never abusing power. This cannot be emphasized too strongly in the formation of seminarians since an abuse of authority and power effectively negates everything else that the priest does.

Conclusion

I have been involved in the training of seminarians, in some capacity, for nearly forty years, both with diocesan seminarians and religious scholastics preparing for the priesthood. I have been involved as well both with their academic formation and their personal spiritual formation. These reflections and suggestions are offered out of that experience. I present them here for discussion, recognizing that my view is not the only one and that my suggestions are incomplete. But I offer them because, after forty years of being involved with seminaries, I feel that we are not in a happy place right now vis-à-vis seminary formation. We are too polarized around many of the issues that are raised in this article. Priests' gatherings expose a huge rift within dioceses and religious orders, and sadly, too many sincere young men are being ordained without being properly prepared to face the challenges in ministry and the personal ups and downs, depressions, angers, inflations, jealousies, bitterness, overwork, and loneliness that will make themselves felt during the marathon years of their ministry. While the elements named in this essay need further exploration and discussion, they offer a starting point for reclaiming the role of seminaries to equip priests for the increasingly complex and demanding ministry that lies before them. May God be with them! Priesthood is a great vocation—and a very demanding one.

Generational Differences

A Crucial Key

Thomas Walters
Professor Emeritus of Religious Education
Saint Meinrad Seminary & School of Theology
St. Meinrad, Indiana

I find students to be less intellectually flexible, more stuck ideologically.
Boomer generation seminary professor
We want the truth. Period. I think we're sick of clever theories that seem to undermine the church.
Millennial generation seminary student

Introduction

Significant differences in attitude between generations, combined with the shifts in church life associated with the experience of the Second Vatican Council, provide another crucial key to understanding the diversity of church life and practice (*National Directory for Catechesis* 34).

Roman Catholic seminaries are experiencing a generational "changing of the guard." Within the next three to five years the majority of those teaching and studying in Catholic seminaries will have no direct experience of either the *Baltimore Catechism* or the "opening of windows" at the Second Vatican Council. This commentary offers the perspective of an emeritus professor of religious education and former seminary academic dean on how this generational transition has impacted and is impacting the teaching/learning process in Roman Catholic seminaries. Hopefully, these comments can serve as a catalyst for insuring a smoother transition from a generation of faculty and students formed and schooled in a "spirit of Vatican II" to a generation shaped and educated in the evangelical spirit of St. John Paul II.

Initiation and Schooling

When considering generational differences, it is helpful to begin by distinguishing between the two traditional means by which cultures and institutions hand on their values and understandings, namely, initiation and schooling.[1] Initiation is by far the stronger of the two. It is contextual. It is education by osmosis. It is the handing on of the stories, traditions, behaviors, and values of the society through modeling. These forms of initiation were how Catholicism was transmitted in the Polish, Irish, French, Italian, German, and other ethnic communities in the United States and how it is handed on to some extent today, particularly in the Hispanic community.[2] The *National Directory for Catechesis* speaks of the importance of the initiating community when it states:

> The Church, the Body of Christ, is both the principal agent of catechesis and the primary recipient of catechesis. In fact, the life of the Church is a kind of catechesis itself. Every individual has the responsibility to grow in faith and to contribute to the growth in faith of the other members of the Church.[3]

Schooling, on the other hand, is a more intentional process with programmatic learning that takes place in structured settings. By its nature, schooling tends to be more highly cognitive and depends upon and flows from a strong and stable initiating environment. This is why the *Baltimore*

---

[1] For a more detailed description see the article by Didier Piveteau, "School, Society and Catechetics," in *Religious Education and the Future*, ed. Dermot Lane, 20–30 (New York: Paulist Press, 1986).

[2] In growing numbers, "Hispanics are transforming the nation's religious landscape, especially the Catholic Church, not only because of their growing numbers but also because they are practicing a distinctive form of Christianity." See The Pew Hispanic Project, "Changing Faiths: Latinos and the Transformation of American Religion," the Pew Forum and Religion and Public Life, Executive Summary, available from http://pewforum.org/surveys/hispanic/ (23 August 2008).

[3] United States Catholic Bishops, *National Directory for Catechesis* (Washington, DC: USCCB, 2005), 186.

Catechism proved for many to be an effective teaching tool by providing activities being modeled in the somewhat stable initiating Catholic community of the time with a shared explanation and vocabulary.

It is a truism that the initiating Catholic community in the United States is not stable. The values and practices the Catholic community now model are diverse and at times contradictory. Chester Gillis wrote in 1999, "The Catholic Church in America, indeed all over the world, has changed more in the past thirty-five years than it had in the previous three and a half centuries."[4] The generations that are the products of this period of instability in Catholic identity are fast becoming the majority of students, faculty, and administrators of today's seminaries. Their presence has changed the nature of theological education in Roman Catholic seminaries. These are the students that Mary Hess describes as experiencing a need for "more sharply bounded religious communities."[5]

Generations

Tom Robinson, the editor of *The Greentree Gazette*, reports, "While race and socio-economics are factors, the year in which one is born can account for twice the effect on personality and behavior as do the parents who raised the child."[6] John Allen reports that James Davidson, who has conducted a number of studies on generational differences within the Catholic Church, argues that generation "should be taken seriously alongside other markers of diversity such as race, gender and class in both academic programming and pastoral ministry."[7]

A generation is a theoretical construct. It is a way to think about and integrate diverse information in an orderly way. It is not a tool for pigeon-holing. Thus it is important to heed the following caution:

---

[4] Chester Gillis, *Roman Catholicism in America* (New York: Columbia University Press, 1999), 26.

[5] Mary Hess, "A New Culture of Learning: What Are the Implications for Theological Education?," *Teaching Theology and Religion* 17, issue 3 (July 2014): 230.

[6] Tom Robinson, "Are you courting Millennials? Be careful what you wish for," *The Greentree Gazette* (March 2008): 50.

[7] John L. Allen Jr., "Young theologians today face 'paranoia,' new Fordham prof says," *National Catholic Reporter*, June 6, 2008, http://ncronline.org/news/young -theologians-today-face-paranoia-new-fordham-prof-says.

Keep in mind that identifying a "generation" is an analytical tool for understanding our culture and the people within it. It simply reflects the idea that people who are born over a certain period of time are influenced by a unique set of circumstances and global events, moral and social values, technologies, and cultural behavioral norms. The result is that every generation has a different way of seeing life. Recognizing the generational concept as a tool, rather than as definitive for every person, means that exceptions are to be expected.[8]

Figure 1

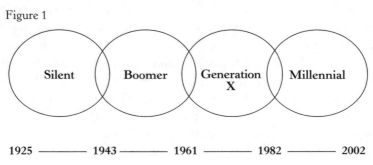

A generation can be understood as a society-wide peer group. It extends for about twenty years and has the following characteristics: a similarity in attitudes toward family life, gender roles, institutions, politics, religion, culture, lifestyle, and perspectives on the future. Not everyone in a generation shares the same opinions, but every member is influenced by the ethos of the times. A generation also tends to be fuzzy at the edges, that is, the closer one is to either end of the generational spectrum the more likely one is to look like the generation that precedes or follows.[9] This fuzziness is represented by the overlapping circles in figure 1. The dates and titles for the four generations are drawn from the research of Howe and Strauss: Silent (born 1925–42), Boomer (1943–60), Generation X (1961–81) and Millennial (1982–2002).[10] Howe and Strauss state:

[8] David Kinnaman and Gabe Lyons, *unChristian: What a New Generation Really Thinks about Christianity* (Grand Rapids, MI: Baker Books, 2007), 17.

[9] Gary L. McIntosh, *One Church, Four Generations* (Grand Rapids, MI: Baker Books, 2007), 199–202.

[10] Dates given for the generations tend to vary. I have chosen the dates used by Howe, Strauss, and Matson in *Generations* (New York: Morrow, 1991), 32. The following website is an excellent starting point for understanding the generations: http://www.fourthturning.com.

> History creates generations, and generations create history. The cycle
> draws forward energy from each generation's need to redefine the
> social role of each new phase of life it enters. And it draws circular
> energy from each generation's tendency to fill perceived gaps and to
> correct (indeed overcorrect) the excesses of its elders.[11]

The generations of theology professors that were raised in the 1950s
and 1960s, a time when one tended to learn the answers without fully
understanding the questions, have found themselves prone to promoting a
more experiential and pastoral approach to theological education. Younger
faculty and seminarians who were the recipients of a catechesis that did
not emphasize doctrinal foundations find themselves advocating for a
theological education that places more emphasis on the fundamentals of
the faith. Doctrinal grounding, they contend, will lead to a more authentic
experience of the love of God and more evangelical fervor.

In general, faculty and students from the end of the Boomer generation
through Generation X and the Millennial generation find themselves more
sympathetic to an apologetic approach to seminary formation and theological education than do their colleagues from the Silent and early Boomer
generations. Millennials, in particular, call for more orthodox teaching
and well-trained "orthodox" ordained and lay ecclesial ministers, based
on their own definition of what constitutes orthodoxy. As a result, there
can be and often is a generational disconnect between theological faculty
from the Silent and Boomer generations who were strongly influenced by
the Second Vatican Council and St. John XXIII and those members of
the faculty who are later Boomers, Generation X, and Millennials who
ground their calling in the life and teachings of St. John Paul II.[12] One
only has to sit with seasoned faculty and then with a group of students
during an election year to experience not only a political but an ecclesial
generational divide.

So, what are the perceived gaps and excesses of their elders that late
Boomers, Xers, and Millennials feel compelled to address? A partial answer
is found in their reflections on their formal religious education.

---

[11] William Strauss and Neil Howe, "F.A.Q., The Fourth Turning, About Our
Message," 1996, http://www.fourthturning.com/html/about_our_message.html.

[12] This disconnect is similar to the tension that has been observed in presbyter-
ates between the Vatican II priests and the more recently ordained "John Paul II"
priests. See Dean R. Hoge and Jacqueline E. Wenger, *Evolving Visions of the Priesthood*
(Collegeville, MN: Liturgical Press, 2003), 61–78.

Looking Back

In a recent national survey of parish catechetical leaders, seminarians, and college students, participants were asked to describe one way in which the generation into which they were born impacted their religious formation.[13] Members of the Silent generation pointed to the strong initiating community in which they grew up and its impact on their ministry, especially the strong value system of the family, parish-centered activities, and Catholic schooling. Although they realize that it is impossible to replicate that era, their experiences of growing up Catholic instilled in them a desire to impart the good aspects of their formation to those they catechize.

Boomers, likewise, referred to the influence of the initiating community in which they grew up, but the changes brought about by Vatican Council II seem to have impacted their catechetical practice even more. They mention their ability to be flexible and to accept change and ambiguity. They view themselves as bridge builders between the pre- and post-Vatican II church, and they eagerly embrace this role. Many of the middle and late Boomers noted that their formal religious education began with the *Baltimore Catechism*, but all they remember of their education beyond adolescence are "balloons and butterflies." As one Boomer put it, "I started out with the *Baltimore Catechism* and ended up with felt-and-burlap banners." In general, Boomers do not see this as negative. Many feel that they have been strengthened and enriched by experiencing both pre- and post-Vatican Council II catechesis. "Roots in the pre-Vatican II and wings from Vatican II. Respect for authority and the understanding we need to question authority. Passion for justice and inclusion. Both/and generation."

Both the Silent and Boomer respondents proudly point to the fact it was not only in their generation but also because of their generations' efforts that lay ministry came into its own. They view this as one of their generations' major achievements. It was during their generations that laymen and laywomen were given the encouragement and freedom to pursue ministry as a career, which resulted in many of them answering the call to serve the church and taking advantage of the opportunity to pursue degrees in religious education and theological studies.

---

[13] See Thomas P. Walters and Rita Tyson Walters, *A Crucial Key: Generational Perspectives and Catechetical Leadership* (Washington, DC: NCEA, 2009).

Having grown up during the civil rights movement, members of the Boomer generation note their dedication to social justice issues and its impact on their catechetical practice. "Though many were 'radical chic' in my generation, I BELIEVE in the peace and love of the 60s and 70s. I BELIEVE in the social justice teachings of Martin Luther King, Jr., and the war protests of the Berrigans." Civil disobedience and questioning authority are viewed and valued by many Boomers as an essential part of living the Christian life.

Unlike their elders, Generation X and Millennials are less likely to speak of a strong initiating community or of Vatican II. For them, the greater impact on their formation was the person and papacy of St. John Paul II, particularly his World Youth Days. In light of what they perceive to be their own experience of weak catechesis, they desire to teach the doctrines of the church to adults and youth alike. Having themselves been formed by a catechesis that emphasized experience over doctrine, these two generations are inclined to give more emphasis to doctrine and ritual over experience. They believe they have a more balanced approach to handing on the faith than do their older colleagues. These are the students and younger faculty who are populating seminary classrooms.

Filling Gaps

Each generation attempts to fill the gaps in the generation that preceded it. Pre- and Vatican II generation Catholics grew up in a religion. Everything was in place to enforce the rules and regulations that defined a good Catholic. There was an ideal to strive for, a bar to be reached. The line between good and bad behavior was clearly defined and publicly proclaimed. A good Catholic toed the line. The gap in their formation was the lack of recognition that faith is a gift to be received, not a command to be obeyed. Faith elicits commitment, not subservience. This is the gap that many pre- and Vatican II Catholics sought to fill. They went in search of the gift of faith rather than the rigors of religion. The following generations of Catholics find themselves lost in place. There seems to be no firm ground to stand on. To them constant searching is a futile enterprise. They believe they possess the gift of faith, and they want it to be concretized.

Representatives of each of these scenarios are found in today's seminary classrooms, often in the roles of teacher and learner and equally convinced of the need to fill their perceived gap, but distrustful that the other can do it. The searcher and the settler in the same space present a unique set of generational challenges for seminary educators and students alike.

Teaching/Learning and Generational Differences

Teaching is an intentional activity designed to make a specific and observable difference in the lives of learners. The teaching/learning act consists of four variables—teacher, learner, subject matter (content), and context (for example, the seminary classroom). How one understands and manipulates each of these integral variables determines the effectiveness of the enterprise. Not surprisingly, the generational characteristics previously described come into play with each of these variables. Ignoring their influence jeopardizes both teaching and learning. Trying to deny, avoid, numb, or eradicate generational differences is neither possible nor desirable. They are an inevitable and necessary part of the teaching/learning process. It is the collision of these differences that can make teaching and learning both frightening and exhilarating. The best teachers realize this and make room for generational differences, allowing them to shape the teaching/learning process. The following principles may help seminary faculty and students use the crucial key of generational differences to unlock the treasure chest of theological studies.

1. Respect and Engage Generational Differences

How we traverse our early years has lasting impact on our religious journey. The same is true of our colleagues and students. Ask yourself what you need to learn about the generational characteristics of your colleagues and students and then share your questions with them. It is as easy as beginning with the question, "What was your experience of growing up Catholic (Lutheran, Baptist, no religion)?" When we learn together to see both the positives and the negatives in each other's formation, we are better able to engage both our students and our colleagues in theological discourse. The Catholic theological tradition, laws, teachings, and rubrics are not ends in themselves, but tools for a journey that changes with each generation. There are no theological concepts that are not shaded with the fog of our inability to totally grasp or to be totally sure. A Boomer faculty member advises, "Listen, listen, listen! Help students to understand that we are all cultural subjects. Ask them: How do you define yourself and who is doing the defining?" Likewise, all faculty members would do well to answer the same two questions for themselves.

2. Nurture Intergenerational Bonding

"Learn about the generations so you can better understand them," says Sharon Jordan-Evans, an executive coach. "Learn about the challenges that shaped their formative years. Those events impact their attitudes, perceptions, values and expectations in life and at work."[14] Don't judge colleagues by their age, appearance, or era—judge them by their commitment and ability to work within the framework of the church's call to hand on the Catholic faith. Whether you are young or old, recognize that your colleague from another generation was formed in a different time and thus views things differently and will result in some differing of opinions. Let your colleagues and students alike know that, despite differences, you are aware of the commitment that they bring to theological study and that you are all drawing from the same source documents and ecclesial tradition.

3. Encourage Conversation

What produces good conversation? It is a topic that the student regards as important, and it is a problem that they want to solve. Don't just discuss readings, but use the readings as starters for engaging the ideas, issues, or problems the readings address. Howard Sandel, a Harvard political theorist, commenting on gaining students' attention and holding it, suggests starting with what "students care about, know, or think they know, rather than just lay out a blueprint or an outline or tale or theory or account of our own."[15] This is particularly the case with this latest generation of seminarians and a growing number of lay students who come with an evangelical fervor and a mistrust of theological inquiry that seems in any way critical of the Catholic Church and her teachings. It is important to affirm their call and allow them to give voice to that which brought them to the seminary in their engagement with the selected content of the course. Critical questioning best follows, rather than leads, into discussion of controversial theological topics.

4. Be Patient with Each Other

Because today's seminary students and faculty and administrators come from the generations that were not particularly satisfied with what

---

[14] Matt Krumrie, "Four Generations Working Together," *Star Tribune* (March 20, 2006).

[15] Cited by Ken Bain, *What College Professors Do Best* (Cambridge: Harvard University Press, 2004), 110.

they received in their own formal religious education, they will bring a different set of questions to the classroom and to pastoral ministry, and it is important to realize that they speak for many in their generation. Defining one's distinctive Catholic identity appears to be a more complex task for those who have grown up in the aftermath of Vatican II than it was for those who grew up in the Catholic Church of the 1950s and 1960s. It is important to recognize this and to support them in their efforts.

On the other hand, younger faculty and administrators must be open to respectful critique from their elders. No one's point of view is *the* point of view on how to most effectively hand on our religious tradition. "A great attitude and open mind toward each other will develop the respect, communication, compassion, and tolerance toward each other to make it seem as if there is no generational gap," says Faye Coffey, cofounder of Minnesota-based Winning Careers.[16]

5. Trust in God and Have a Sense of Humor

"Imagine walking into a room that is evenly populated between kindergartners and forty-year-olds. Now try and say something that *everybody* will find funny. That's what today's workforce is like."[17] This is part of a comedy routine by Greg Schwem on the humorous side of generational differences. His image of a diversely populated room captures what we see whenever theological faculty and administrators gather. It is also what we see when parishes gather. As a result, there is no one approach to sharing the light of our faith tradition that *everybody* is going to find appropriate and convincing. Apparently, this is the way God intended it to be. But we are not without hope. "As the Church embarks upon a new millennium of life in Christ, the power of the Holy Spirit invigorates her universal mission to proclaim the name of Jesus Christ boldly and to bear witness to him courageously throughout the whole world. His promise to accompany his disciples 'until the end of the age' propels our journey in faith, gives us reason for the hope that is in us, and ensures the fulfillment of our mission."[18]

American cartoonist Charles M. Schulz is quoted as saying, "If I were given the opportunity to present a gift to the next generation, it would be

---

[16] Krumrie, "Four Generations Working Together."
[17] Greg Schwem, "Generational Humor Crash," August 20, 2007.
[18] *National Directory for Catechesis*, 297.

the ability for each individual to learn to laugh at him[/her]self." Trusting in the Holy Spirit as the reason for their hope, seminary leaders and theological faculty have no excuse for not developing this ability. Seminary formation and the theological enterprise are too important not to have a sense of humor.

Conclusion

We must never forget that what is familiar to us can be strange and difficult to colleagues and students of a different generation. Teaching and learning go together; both require inquisitiveness, self-discovery, hard work, and the willingness to be self-critical. When we were born, where we were born, and the experiences surrounding our growing up not only shape our identity but also influence our vision and tactics. They are our generational "mini-narratives" that always travel with us. As a result, we have a professional responsibility to reflect critically on our generational tendencies and biases and to be aware of how they impact our approach to our discipline as well as to our instructional design and study habits. God placed us all in the exact moment in time where he wanted us to be; now it is up to each of us, professor and student alike, to take advantage of the crucial key of generational differences in our efforts to teach and to learn effectively in the theological disciplines.

For Reflection and Conversation

1. Describe in some detail the generation in which you grew up.
2. When it comes to religion, how are you alike or different from your generational cohorts?
3. What was the generational impact on your religious formation?
4. What gaps are you trying to fill?
5. How has growing up in your generation impacted your approach to your discipline? your approach to instruction?
6. If you are a student, how has growing up in your generation impacted your religious thinking and your expectations in a theology classroom?

Human Formation

Fostering Happy, Healthy, and Holy Ministers to Be a Bridge to Christ in Service to God's People

Leon M. Hutton
Vice-Rector and Director of Human Formation
and Evaluations (to 2015)
St. John's Seminary, Camarillo, California

The Second Vatican Council addressed the issue of priestly formation with two key documents: *Optatam Totius* (*OT*; Decree on the Training of Priests) and *Presbyterorum Ordinis* (*PO*; Decree on the Ministry and Life of Priests). The first, *OT*, affirmed the centrality of spiritual formation as the foundation upon which intellectual and pastoral formation is based. Because priests take on the likeness of Christ the High Priest, they should "learn to cling to him as friends by intimately sharing their entire lives with him" (*OT* 8). The second document acknowledged the increasing expectations of the priest to serve in the likeness of Christ the Teacher, Priest, and King and share in his ministry and they are to "establish and increase the people of God" (*PO* 4). *Lumen Gentium* (*LG*; Dogmatic Constitution on the Church) went on to affirm the identity of the priest as the image of Christ, sharing in the unique office of Christ, the mediator (*LG* 28). In the years that followed, these documents set the agenda for the work of priestly formation.

Seminary formation programs attempted to meet the needs of seminarians and the expectations of their bishops, religious superiors, vocation directors, and the local church. Faculty and staff brought their specific expertise as teachers and formators to the work of priestly formation on a variety of levels. These academic ecclesial communities integrated a wide range of formational components and experiences in order to prepare healthy and spiritually astute pastoral leaders for the church.

Since Vatican II, several documents have contributed to the concepts that are to guide seminary formation. *Ratio Fundamentalis Institutionis Sacerdotalis* (1970, revised 1985) outlines the basic program of formation and the *PPF*, now in its fifth edition, articulates the basic standards for all seminaries in the United States. Each revision has reflected the ongoing improvement of formation programs by responding to the shifting trends and needs of church and society. Seminaries have sought to maintain a high quality of professionalism in all aspects of formation by following these directives.

The synod of bishops met in 1990 on "The Formation of Priests in Circumstances of the Present Day" to review the state of seminary formation and the nature of the priesthood in light of the changing needs of seminary candidates. The synod identified the cultural trends affecting those who seek to spread the Gospel, which were reiterated in *PDV*:

> Society is increasingly witnessing a powerful thirst for justice and peace; a more lively sense that humanity must care for creation and respect nature; a more open search for truth; a greater effort to safeguard human dignity; a growing commitment in many sectors of the world population to a more specific international solidarity and a new ordering of the world in freedom and justice. (6)

The same synod also noted the problematic elements that impact society, the church, and priestly formation in particular, which appear again in *PDV*. "Rationalism is still very widespread and, in the name of a reductive concept of 'science,' it renders human reason insensitive to an encounter with revelation and with divine transcendence" (*PDV* 7). Along with individualism and personal subjectivism, John Paul II says that it frustrates the capacity for true human relationships. Resulting from these trends emerge forms of compensation that foster a lifestyle of hedonism, materialism, and self-deception that comes from a subjectivism in matters of faith and morality. He states that religious indifference leads to relativism in the doctrine of faith and often a conditional sense of belonging to the church. Alienation from the spiritual foundations once based on family and church adversely impacts vocations and weakens their capacity to be

Christian witnesses and promote evangelization.[1] The pope recognized that seminary formation must address these trends so as to serve the realities of the seminary community and also to support the work of preparing effective ministers to speak to the "signs of the times."

PDV had an immediate impact on seminary formation by highlighting the human qualities necessary for candidates today. It stated clearly that the priest is called to be the "'living image' of Jesus Christ, head and shepherd of the Church, and to seek to reflect in himself, as far as possible, the human perfection which shines forth in the incarnate Word of God" (*PDV* 43). The priest, as the image of Christ, is best reflected in his relationship to his people:

> So we see that the human formation of the priest shows its special importance when related to the receivers of the mission: In order that his ministry may be humanly as credible and acceptable as possible, it is important that the priest should mold *his human personality in such a way that it becomes a bridge and not an obstacle for others in their meeting with Jesus Christ the Redeemer of humanity.* (*PDV* 43; italics added)

Subsequent events have intensified efforts by all those interested in the preparation of seminarians to meet modern challenges: the decline in the number of Catholic priests, the sexual abuse scandal, financial and educational concerns, and the impact of social trends affecting the future of religious life in the United States.

This commentary addresses the movement in seminary formation following the issuance of *PDV* in 1992, which comments extensively on human formation as an essential and explicit component in the overall program of priestly formation. As a result, the fourth edition of the *PPF* in the same year made human formation normative for all seminaries in the United States. Seminary administrations and faculty responded to this initiative by incorporating new dimensions into their formation programs. Study and reflection, seminars and institutes, the 2008 Apostolic Visitation of seminaries, and other professional gatherings of seminary personnel have all advanced the work of human formation.

John Paul II envisioned human formation as the necessary foundation of priestly formation, centered in Jesus Christ, so that the humanity of the priest is instrumental in mediating the redemptive gifts of Christ to people

---

[1] Based on *PDV* 7 and 51.

today. The interplay of all the dimensions is enhanced by a candidate who is "balanced . . . strong and free, capable of bearing the weight of pastoral responsibilities" (*PDV* 43). The publication of the fifth edition of the *PPF* (2005) reflected the great strides that had been made since 1992 to identify the qualities, norms, and virtues associated with human formation and develop the criteria by which seminary candidates and formation faculty could assess progress in this aspect of formation (see *PPF* 74–86).

A Brief Overview of Formation: Based on the Example of St. John's Seminary, California

Like every seminary, St. John's possesses a distinctive personality due to its location, episcopal and religious leadership, history and traditions, specific mission, and cultural and ethnic makeup. Rooted in the Vincentian tradition of seminary formation, St. John's was staffed by them from 1939 to 1965. The seminary handbook of 1940 centered the qualities of priestly formation on the virtues of discipline and piety. During this period, most seminarians came with a strong Catholic cultural identity passed on through the family, parish, and parochial education. They matriculated through the minor seminary system and were well prepared for the rigors of the major seminary. Therefore, the program of "human" formation emphasized the practice of discipline as described in the seminary rules, and required order, regularity, and good conduct. The 1940 St. John's catalogue stated,

> The written rules are few and simple, and are such as the priest should try to observe in his after life on the mission. Their observance accustoms the student to regularity of life, self-restraint, to proper regard for their companions and to prompt and cheerful obedience to authority. (20)

Accordingly, a seminarian's demonstration of priestly qualities reflected self-discipline, attention to duty, self-control, and obedience to authority and were the basis for measuring a candidate's suitability. Sufficient intellectual ability and observance of the seminary's spiritual exercises were additional indicators.[2]

---

[2] SJS Catalogue, 21. The seminary program highlighted special devotions to the mysteries of the incarnation and the Holy Eucharist, to the Blessed Mother of God, especially under the title of Her Immaculate Conception, to St. Joseph, patron and

Students found guidance in the help of a spiritual director and confessor as "God's appointed representative to guide them in the way of true spirituality." Along with the other seminary faculty, these appointed representatives served as mentors and also contributed to creating a culture of evaluation. Seminarians were expected to implicitly trust the faculty's judgment about their vocational discernment. Seminary rules spoke of sanctions or punishments that might result in being delayed or dismissed from the formation program. In some cases, the absolute determination by the seminary administration over the lives of the seminarians gave little credence to the seminarian's discernment. It also fostered a climate of mistrust and deception among some who struggled with the culture of formation.

From 1966 to 1976, inspired by Vatican II documents, the programs changed language and emphasis. At St. John's in 1966, for example, the seminary handbook continued to speak of duty and self-restraint, but added a spirit of regard for companions and cheerful obedience to authority. It included a statement that encouraged "a spirit of honor and gentlemanliness." Sanctions delineating grounds for punishment and dismissal were omitted. More significantly, the function of the seminary was "to form students to piety and personal sanctity according to the model, Jesus Christ, as He is Teacher, Priest and Shepherd."[3]

The expanding vision of professional priestly formation envisioned by Vatican II enhanced all aspects of the formation program. The first edition of the *PPF* became the standard for priestly formation. By 1972 there was a significant shift in language and direction in the formation program. The language of order, duty, and obedience to authority was replaced, giving candidates "the opportunity to exercise personal responsibility in the use of freedom, the role of authority in community life, and the value of self-discipline and personal growth for service to the community." The progress of a formation program that now emphasized responsibility and freedom, self-discipline, and growth for service placed the seminarian in a different relationship to the formation process. This was a major transition

---

protector of the church universal, to St. John the apostle and evangelist (titular patron of the seminary), and to the great model of priestly Catholic action, St. Vincent de Paul. Finally, recognizing the absolute necessity of unswerving loyalty and devotion on the part of the priest of the Vicar of Christ and obedience to his every injunction are strongly inculcated.

[3] SJS Catalogue (1966), 16. This same language is reflected in *PO* 13.

from the expectation of conformity and obedience and compliance to duty and authority. The formation program now emphasized personal responsibility, growth in accountability and maturity, and lives imitating Jesus Christ.

At the same time "spiritual formation" replaced the previous heading of "piety and spiritual guidance." A comprehensive approach to spirituality integrally connected formation for priestly ministry and personal holiness. The section states: "A program of direction and counseling exists to ensure that the diverse elements of seminary training—academic instruction, pastoral field education, community life and discipline—will achieve a vital synthesis with the personal life of the student."[4] Seminary faculty worked toward this synthesis by meeting with students in small groups (external forum) and one-on-one (internal forum).

By 1977, the mission statement expanded its scope:

> [We] prepare men, who believe that they are called by God, to be priests in the Roman Catholic Church. In our understanding, a priest may be described as a disciple called to be a builder (facilitator-enabler) of community through the ministry of the sacraments, especially the Eucharist, and of the Word.[5]

Priesthood was, therefore, not a function but an identity, a sacramental conformity to Christ. This call was realized through the indwelling of the Spirit and affirmed by the church in order to be a builder and servant of the community in Christ. The purpose of the seminary was to aid men in "their personal growth to be mature Christians." While spiritual formation continued to hold principal emphasis in the life of seminarians, the means to achieve personal growth was nurtured and integrated through the other aspects of formation. Personal, academic, and pastoral formation began to play a more supportive role in the overall formation process. The program of personal formation sought to develop mature candidates who could deepen their relationship with God and others. The program focused on growth in Christian maturity, personal responsibility and group relationships, awareness and understanding of cultures, social consciousness and communication skills, and the ability to live and foster the life of the Christian community.

---

[4] SJS Catalogue (1972), 19.
[5] SJS Catalogue (1977), 8.

In the 1980s, some seminaries focused more on the spiritual dimension of formation. St. John's, for example, began a two-month intensive period of spiritual formation for first-year theology students. Its purpose was to expose candidates to the treasures of the Catholic spiritual tradition and deepen their appreciation of how these traditions play out in devotional life. This experience focused on the human qualities necessary for those who sought an integrated life of prayer, reflection, and communal living. Developing practical life skills was a component of the program and was expressed in the use of group theological reflection and leadership formation, manual labor, and communal life skills.

Practical implementation of the virtue of charity and the appreciation of other faith traditions received new emphasis. Among other essential components were growing in knowledge and acceptance of one's gifts and limitations, developing trust and a mature attitude toward human sexuality, and embracing a celibate life, poverty, and authority. In 1987, a celibacy formation module was initiated for first-year theology students, providing workshops and programs on various aspects of celibate chastity. This module was facilitated by faculty advisers and a team of older seminarians who acted as group facilitators and presenters.

With the focus on forming diocesan priests for service in the culturally diverse southwestern United States, St. John's looked to prepare culturally competent candidates attuned to the growing Hispanic population and the new immigrants from Asian countries. This vision of the future acknowledged that "the Church as a human institution is constantly growing and maturing and the makeup of communities is changing."[6] The ability and desire for seminary candidates to embrace the capacity for intercultural competency became an important dimension of the program. By the beginning of the 1990s, seminary formation programs were responding to the ever-increasing responsibilities and demands being placed on seminarians.

Human Formation: The Basis of All Priestly Formation

Influenced by *PDV* and *PPF* IV, human formation took on greater importance. A director was appointed and charged with identifying how the formation program would assist seminarians to become a "bridge and not an obstacle for others in their meeting with Jesus Christ the

[6] SJS Catalogue (1977), 10.

Redeemer of humanity" (*PDV* 43). The purpose of human formation at St. John's emphasized the development of these human qualities: "love of truth, loyalty, respect for all persons, justice, honesty and good balance in judgement and behavior. Of special importance is the affective ministry, the capacity to give and receive friendship and love, as well as the ability to relate well to others."[7]

These objectives and the methods to achieve them were not only new, but at times confusing for seminarians and faculty. The role of spiritual directors had a long and established history working in the "internal forum" where confidentiality about matters of conscience were strictly observed. At the same time, there were now human formation advisers who worked in the "external forum" with candidates on behavioral characteristics associated with growth in the active virtues necessary for effective priestly ministry. What *PDV* proposed was a deeper, more intense preparation and evaluation of the seminarians' capacity for development of the necessary human qualities for ministry. Consequently, education of the entire seminary community in the application of the vision described in *PDV* effected a cultural change in formation.

Ongoing Development of Seminary Formation: Renewing Seminary Life

Throughout the late 1990s and early 2000s, consultation among those entrusted with seminary formation programs prepared the way for the fifth edition of *PPF*.[8] The revision, especially of the section on human formation, benefited from a broad consultation with bishops, religious superiors, the community of seminary formators, and numerous professional organizations. Utilizing this experience and the expertise of its formation faculty, St. John's continued to make progress in developing a comprehensive program to meet the formational needs of its seminarians. The challenges of seminary formation required the ongoing preparation of the formation faculty to develop skills, expertise, and commitment to wisely and prudently assess the readiness of seminarians for ministry.

---

[7] *Seminary Formation Handbook* (1994–95), 24.

[8] The bishops' Committee on Priestly Formation began the revision of the *PPF* in 2001. Along with the influence of *PDV*, the document also credits other papal documents that shaped the vision of priestly formation: *Novo Millennio Ineunte* (2001) and *Ecclesia in America* (1999), as well as earlier ecclesial documents.

An important development in the formation process was reflected in the annual review experience. Prior to the publication of the fifth edition of the *PPF*, every seminarian had the guidance and support of an external formation adviser who met with him to prepare for his annual review. The outcome of the exercise was then presented to the faculty, who offered impressions and concerns about the seminarian's advancement in the program. The formation adviser acted as an "advocate" on behalf of the seminarian. After the evaluation process, the faculty voted for advancement or dismissal of the seminarian. For the most part, the wisdom of the faculty as a whole, based on their personal impressions and experience of the seminarian, was the main criterion utilized to determine the readiness and viability of the seminarian for advancement.

Since the publication of the latest *PPF*, the external formation adviser has taken a more active role. More time is given to meetings with the seminarian to discuss issues that pertain to questions and themes in human formation. The external formation adviser is viewed less as an advocate and more as a companion supporting the seminarian's growth in the human qualities necessary for ministry. This relationship of trust and care is meant to support the seminarian's ongoing discernment as reflected in the writing of the annual review. Handbooks offer a template of that self-evaluation and present the significant aspects of areas for growth that the seminarian must consider along with a number of other topics for reflection that might help in his personal assessment.[9] This process respects the growth of each individual seminarian and encourages his vocational discernment as an ecclesial experience.[10]

---

[9] The Human Formation Handbook and the Seminary Rule of Life were a combined effort to support the discernment of the seminarians. The Handbook provided the seminarian with step-by-step instructions about the annual review process and the means to personally assess their growth through reflection questions and a Criteria for Growth by which they could measure the seminary's expectations for growth by their formation level or year. The Formation Handbook was regularly revised year after year to reflect the ongoing development and growth being made in the Human Formation Program.

[10] The annual review experience was based on the seminarian's personal reflection or self-assessment of his formation goals and insights along with evaluation documents from pastoral placements, summer programs, participation in seminary community, academic progress, and peer reviews. Those present during the review included the seminarian, his formation adviser, and a team of three faculty members. Observers included the spiritual director and the vocation director or diocesan representative.

The impact of the sexual abuse crisis has made a deep impression on the church and society, vocational recruitment, and seminary programs. The Vatican-mandated visitation of seminaries set out to assess all aspects of the formation program with special emphasis on spiritual and human formation, including formation in human sexuality and maturity, celibacy and the evangelical counsels, and Catholic moral teaching. The abuse crisis presented the seminary community with a renewed determination to address areas of personal growth and development in seminarians in all aspects of the formation program. Many seminarians responded with openness and cooperated fully in this renewal effort.

To embrace a holistic and comprehensive approach to celibacy formation, St. John's expanded its program by instituting the St. John Vianney Conferences, which took to heart the exhortation of John Paul II and the principles presented in the *PPF* to incorporate the evangelical counsels—chaste celibacy, obedience, and simplicity of life—into the formation curriculum. The entire seminary community annually participated in various dimensions of integrating the evangelical counsels into its life as a community.[11] In addition, the conferences of the rector and seminary spiritual director frequently addressed this theme.

Finally, growing in cultural awareness and sensitivity must be evident in the classroom, in the many religious and cultural celebrations of the seminarians, and in daily community life. Growth in cultural competency and developing the skills to minister in a multicultural church are explored through language immersion experiences and other consciousness-raising events as well. A year-long internship experience offers seminarians a challenging experience of diversity. In many ways, the program of human formation at St. John's embodies the vision of the *PPF* by consistently preparing seminarians to be instruments of Christ's grace by displaying such qualities as freedom, maturity, prudence, being men of communion, possessing affective maturity, and capable of being a public person (*PPF* V 76).

---

[11] Each level of formation was tasked with a deeper reflection on the counsels. Pre-theology students were offered a general overview of seminary formation and discernment in light of the counsels. Theology I and IV focused on chaste celibacy. Theology II seminarians reflected on obedience and Theology III seminarians on simplicity of life.

Collaboration of Seminary and Professional Organizations

St. John's has benefited from recent efforts to collaborate with many organizations that specialize in promoting the work of seminary formation and human development. These include the recently formed National Association of Catholic Theological Schools (NACTS), the Institute for Seminary Formators conducted by the Sulpicians, and the professional associations for spiritual directors, academic deans, and pastoral formation faculty. Saint Luke Institute has offered educational opportunities and workshops, along with professional assessment of seminary applicants, in order to support the seminary's efforts to provide formators with the tools to give candidates the spiritual and psychological insights needed to grow in their human development, sexual identity, and affective maturity. Saint Luke's is partnering with seminaries to develop an effective curriculum for human formation that facilitates a balanced program, acknowledges the limitations of the formation faculty, and yet offers the skills needed to be an effective listener and mentor.

Conclusion

It is impossible to predict what changes to the formation of seminarians for priestly ministry will take place in the future. Theologates have responded to the many shifts and challenges throughout their history with resilience, creativity, and a fidelity to their mission to prepare ministers in service to the needs of the church. All aspects of seminary formation are a collaborative effort of formators and seminarians along with all who are invested in the program. Most significantly, the *PPF* affirms, "the foundation and center of all human formation is Jesus Christ, the Word made flesh. In his fully developed humanity, he was truly free and with complete freedom gave himself totally for the salvation of the world" (74). Time after time, the movement of the Spirit in people's lives has brought them to discern God's will for them. Sometimes it might mean receiving the call to priestly ministry. At other times, it may be a call to a vocation in another way of life, but always with the hope that it leads to being fully human, fully alive.

Trends in Scripture Study
and Preaching Preparation
in Roman Catholic Seminaries

Barbara E. Reid, OP
Vice President and Academic Dean
Professor of New Testament Studies
Catholic Theological Union, Chicago

It is the first task of priests . . . to preach the Gospel of God to all.

Presbyterorum Ordinis 4

The quality of preaching in Roman Catholic parishes is of critical importance. It ranks only behind an open, welcoming spirit as what most attracts people to their parishes.[1] Pope Francis's recent comments on preaching capture the situation well: "We know that the faithful attach great importance to it, and that both they and their ordained ministers suffer because of homilies: the laity from having to listen to them and the clergy from having to preach them! . . . The homily can actually be an intense and happy experience of the Spirit, a consoling encounter with God's word, a constant source of renewal and growth" (*EG* 135). Since

---

[1] Tied with the quality of preaching is the overall quality of the liturgy. These findings were reported in March 2013 in "Views from the Pews: Parishioner Evaluations of Parish Life in the United States," by Mark M. Gray, Mary L. Gautier, and Melissa A. Cidade, a joint project of five Catholic national ministry organizations funded by The Lilly Endowment. The research was conducted by CARA. For the full report see http://cara.georgetown.edu/staff/webpages/Parishioners%20Phase%20Three.pdf.

Vatican II, Scripture-based preaching has been emphasized as the primary duty of priests (*PO* 4),[2] making formation of excellent preachers one of the primary tasks in seminary education.

This is no small task. Seminary professors report that many seminarians come with little knowledge of Scripture and a spirituality that is not biblically based. Some seminarians are more at home with the *Catechism of the Catholic Church* than the Bible. Some rely on fundamentalist approaches to the Bible while others lean toward apologetic preaching that emphasizes doctrine and dogma. Still, seminary professors also report that their students generally recognize the importance of Scripture for their future work as priests and preachers and are eager to learn more about the Bible and preaching. Seminarians appreciate the role that good preaching has played in their own lives, and they aim to be of service to the Gospel by doing the same for others.[3] This commentary, based on research with seminary faculty, remarks on ten trends in Scripture study and preaching in Roman Catholic seminaries, and poses questions about their implications for the future.

1. The Place of Biblical Studies and Homiletics in the Seminary Curriculum

Scripture study continues to have a prominent place in the curriculum in the United States seminaries. The number of Scripture courses required for ordination candidates has remained fairly steady for the past thirty years. On average eighteen credits are now required covering introduction to the Bible, methodology, prophets, Psalms, Wisdom literature, Synoptic

---

[2] See also *Dei Verbum* (Dogmatic Constitution on Divine Revelation), which asserts, "all the preaching of the Church must be nourished and ruled by Sacred Scripture" (21).

[3] These comments and others throughout this essay are taken from responses to a survey I sent to ninety-eight professors of Scripture and forty-five professors of homiletics at thirty-eight seminaries in the United States and the North American College in Rome in October 2014. A total of fifty-one responses were received from thirty-three professors of Scripture and eighteen professors of homiletics from twenty-nine institutions. I wish to express my deep gratitude to Sr. Katarina Schuth and her assistant, Catherine Slight, who compiled lists of seminary personnel and their email addresses, and to Richard Mauney, director of Educational Technology at Catholic Theological Union, who prepared the survey instrument and compiled the results.

Gospels, Pauline letters, and Johannine literature.[4] Scripture courses average slightly more than 15 percent of the curriculum.

It is impossible to cover the whole Bible in detail within the required courses. Biblical professors aim to introduce students to the content and theology of particular books of the Bible, developing the requisite skills to study books not included in the curriculum. Students are encouraged as well to take biblical courses as electives and to incorporate ongoing biblical study as integral to their priestly ministry.

Almost all seminaries report preparation of preachers as a stated goal of the curriculum. Ordination candidates in most seminaries must take from two to four preaching courses. In addition, it is common to ask students in other courses, especially those in Scripture, to draw implications of course material for preaching. Since preaching is an art that must be practiced in order to grow and deepen one's abilities, seminaries generally have their students preach at some of the liturgies.

2. Integration and Interdisciplinary Collaboration

For any candidate for ordination, preaching is the ultimate act of integration of his study, prayer, ministry, and life experience. Integration is complex and students need help in learning how to move from exegetical study of the biblical text to proclamation of the Word. Too often, students revert to piety so that theological and biblical study is hardly evident in their homilies. Some tend to latch on to a word or phrase in the text and use that as a springboard for reflection that has little correspondence to the theology or message of the biblical text. Another tendency is to lapse into moralizing.[5]

One of the ways seminary faculty help students integrate more effectively is through interdisciplinary collaboration. In many seminaries, biblical faculty members have a role in assessing the competence of students in preaching, and in some seminaries all faculty evaluate homilies preached at liturgies. A number of schools offer courses that are team-taught by Bible

---

[4] The fifth edition of the *PPF* also designates that study of the Pentateuch, Historical Books, Acts, and Catholic Epistles be required.

[5] These tendencies were evident in a study of newly ordained graduates of Roman Catholic seminaries carried out in 1994–98 by my colleague Leslie Hoppe, OFM, and me. For a copy of the report *Preaching from the Scriptures: New Directions for Preparing Preachers*, contact breid@ctu.edu.

and preaching professors. In some seminaries, where the same professor teaches both Scripture and homiletics, integration happens naturally.

Scripture professors guide students in making homiletic applications in a variety of ways. Some require seminarians to prepare homilies on the biblical texts rather than write formal exegetical papers, showing how their exegeses inform the homily. Others require that every exegesis paper have a section describing a homiletic or other pastoral application. Many facilitate classroom discussions around the question, "How would you preach this text?" Other Scripture professors regularly use class time to work with students on the Sunday Lectionary readings.

3. Academic Study Based on Critical Biblical Methods

Seminary professors observe that a number of their students do not seem to be very academically inclined. In addition, many second-career seminarians have not had adequate undergraduate studies in philosophy, theology, or liberal arts. The learning curve is steep, and, as one homiletics professor commented, "Some think they can get by in their preaching with pious thoughts and generalizations."

Almost every seminary teaches students historical-critical and literary-critical methods of biblical study. More than half of seminary Bible professors also teach the spiritual sense and the use of rhetorical-critical and sociocultural approaches to the text. About one-third of those surveyed introduce students to feminist approaches to the Bible. A few include liberationist, postcolonial, structural, theological, reader-response, intertextual, canonical, and medieval (literal, allegorical, moral, anagogical) approaches. Others expose their students to the reception history of the text and to rabbinic and patristic commentaries. Some faculty observe, however, that some seminarians resist historical-critical approaches, and some report outright hostility toward feminist interpretations.

In their 1993 document "The Interpretation of the Bible in the Church," the Pontifical Biblical Commission described and evaluated six different approaches to biblical interpretation and several subcategories under each method: (a) historical-critical; (b) new methods of literary analysis (including rhetorical, narrative, and semiotic); (c) approaches based on tradition (canonical, Jewish traditions of interpretation, history of the influence of the text); (d) approaches that use human sciences (sociological, cultural anthropology, psychological and psychoanalytic); (e) contextual approaches (liberationist, feminist); and (f) fundamentalist interpretation.

The document found that all but the last approach contribute something valuable for the use of the Scriptures in the life of the church.

Teaching seminarians contemporary critical methods of biblical study opens up the text in ways that enhance the understanding of the preacher. It is especially important that seminarians be exposed to interpretations of Scripture by those whose context may be different from their own, for example, commentaries by scholars who are African-American, Hispanic, Asian, Native American, et cetera. Studying work by feminist biblical scholars can also help seminarians understand women's realities and perspectives and learn how to avoid reinforcing sexism from the pulpit. A preacher who has not been introduced to feminist biblical interpretation may unwittingly feed cycles of violence toward women. Seminarians should also study works by Jewish biblical scholars, who can help them understand Jesus as a first-century Jew and avoid anti-Judaism in their preaching.

4. A Love of Scripture and a Biblically Based Spirituality

Seminary professors see a strong interest among their students in the Scriptures as the foundation of their prayer life, particularly with *lectio divina*. Pope Francis affirms the use of *lectio divina* as a way for the preacher to allow himself to be transformed by the Spirit:

> This prayerful reading of the Bible is not something separate from the study undertaken by the preacher to ascertain the central message of the text; on the contrary, it should begin with that study and then go on to discern how that same message speaks to his own life. The spiritual reading of a text must start with its literal sense. Otherwise we can easily make the text say what we think is convenient, useful for confirming us in our previous decisions, suited to our own patterns of thought. Ultimately this would be tantamount to using something sacred for our own benefit and then passing on this confusion to God's people. (*EG* 152)

5. Engaging Diverse Cultures in Preaching

In our increasingly multicultural church, seminary faculty members are more and more attentive to preparing their students to engage diverse cultures in their preaching.[6] Some do so by offering particular courses

---

[6] Attending to the multicultural realities of the congregation is part of what Pope Francis calls "An Ear to the People" (*EG* 154–55).

with an intercultural focus, for example, "Preaching in the Americas" or "Multicultural Homiletics." Others have students preach in a language other than English. In most seminaries, understanding diverse cultures is addressed in several areas of the curriculum. Some seminaries require students to learn Spanish and/or to participate in an immersion program to learn about issues of culture and language. A number of seminaries offer travel study programs in the biblical lands, which not only enriches the students' understanding of Scripture, but also of the ancient and contemporary cultures of those lands. In most seminaries, the student body is culturally diverse, so intercultural awareness is high and is an emphasis in all courses. In light of all this, diversifying the seminary faculty itself has become a pressing challenge.

6. An Interesting Talk vs. Proclamation of Good News

New preachers struggle to arrive at the kind of integration necessary to be able to make, as one homiletics professor put it, "a powerful connection between a revelatory word proclaimed in our midst that calls us to table and mission." He continued, "What we get is often an interesting idea or exegesis, a 'talk' and not a kerygmatic proclamation." Another observed that his students tend to have "a very superficial academic application of the Scriptures, a pedestrian association of the Scriptures to the human condition and relationship with God, a tendency to cosmetically associate everything to the Eucharist and at times default to some type of trusting association of the theme they have drawn out from the readings and pastoral situation with Mary." Another observed a trend toward "a more apologetic style of preaching, one which emphasizes doctrine, dogma, and the catechism," along with "homilies that center upon how Catholicism is under attack by the 'culture.'"

The tension between "an interesting talk" and "proclamation" finds clarity in the approach advocated by Pope Francis, who characterizes the homily as a "dialogue between God and his people" (*EG* 137). He emphasizes the spirit of love that undergirds the dialogue (*EG* 139) and admonishes against "a preaching which would be purely moralistic or doctrinaire or one which turns into a lecture on biblical exegesis," which "detracts from this heart-to-heart communication which takes place in the homily" (*EG* 142). Pope Francis stresses how crucial it is for the preacher to know, understand, and love the congregation with whom he is in dialogue. He also noted, "Dialogue is much more than the communication of a truth. It arises from the enjoyment of speaking and it enriches those who express their love for one another through the medium of words" (*EG* 142). He stressed that the homily is to be positive in tone, which "always offers hope, points to the future, does not leave us trapped in negativity" (*EG* 159).

7. Strengthening Preaching Input and Feedback

Preaching can become a very solitary endeavor. Some of the best preachers, however, solicit regular input from others both in the preparation of the homily and after it is preached. One model is to establish a diverse group of parishioners who commit themselves for a period of time to studying the upcoming Sunday Scriptures and sharing with the preacher how the texts speak to them. The group also gives feedback to the preacher on the previous Sunday's homily. The late Kenneth Untener, bishop of Saginaw, Michigan, from 1980 to 2004, developed another model. Each week he met with four priests and one lay preacher, each of whom submitted a tape of a homily delivered before a congregation. Copies of each tape were distributed to the other members of the group. The homilies were also examined by a professional writer for style. Participation in the process was mandatory for all preachers in the diocese. The evaluation sessions focused on two questions: "How did you experience the word of God in the homily?" and "What difference will this word of God make in your life?"

8. The Potential Contributions of Lay Preaching

Many Roman Catholic seminaries and schools of theology prepare laywomen and laymen for full-time ministry, many of whom have the gift of preaching. They do the requisite theological study and have the spiritual formation and ministerial experience needed to preach well. However, the preaching of the homily at Mass, which is where the majority of Roman Catholics experience the breaking open of the Word, is for the most part restricted to ordained male presbyters and deacons.[7] There are circumstances in which laypersons are allowed to preach the homily, as in liturgies for young children,[8] and there are other forms of preaching, for

---

[7] Code of Canon Law, c. 767 §1.

[8] See Code of Canon Law, c. 766 and the *Directory for Masses with Children* issued by the Sacred Congregation for Divine Worship (Nov. 1, 1973), 24.

example, preaching at non-eucharistic liturgies or catechetical preaching, which laypersons may do.

An important question for the future is whether the pressing pastoral needs and the right of the faithful to hear the Word proclaimed in their own language will open the way for a new norm whereby qualified lay ministers may preach the homily at Mass. In saying "in their own language," I mean not only one's mother tongue, but also one's sociocultural context. Many women, for example, long to hear the Word proclaimed from a woman's perspective—a gift to both men and women in the church.

9. Prioritizing Preaching Preparation in the Face of New Models of Pastoring

With a shortage of priests in many areas of the country, a growing trend has one priest serving multiple parishes, placing more and more administrative and pastoral demands on his time. Many priests find that the lengthy homily preparation process they were taught in the seminary is not possible in such contexts. Recognizing the difficulties, Pope Francis nonetheless urges preachers to devote prolonged time to study, prayer, reflection, and pastoral creativity each week, even if less time has to be given to other important activities. He insists, "A preacher who does not prepare is not 'spiritual'; he is dishonest and irresponsible with the gifts he has received" (*EG* 145).

10. Use of Media in Preaching

Finally, the forms in which the Word is proclaimed and heard are exploding with the proliferation of digital communication. Many preachers now use websites, blogs, tweets, Facebook, and other such media to proclaim the Word. A challenge for seminary professors is to develop courses to help their students learn how to use digital media arts for their ministries, including preaching. It may be that the younger students will have more to teach their professors in this area than vice versa!

Conclusion

The proclamation of the Word remains at the center of priestly ministry. Research on the topic is reassuring. Seminaries take very seriously their obligation to prepare effective preachers, using an array of contemporary critical methods. When Scripture and homiletics faculty collaborate and keep the question of preaching central, the students' ability to integrate theological and biblical study into proclamation of a hope-filled word expands dramatically. Seminaries work hard at fostering in their students a lifelong love of study and prayer with the Word. Seminary faculties help students deepen in their ability to hear the questions, concerns, joys, and sorrows of the people with whom they minister in their own language and culture. They lead students to understand the nature of a homily, so that as preachers they will give a hope-filled kerygmatic proclamation rather than an interesting pious talk or a doctrinal exposition. They encourage future preachers to seek input and receive feedback on their homilies on a regular and formal basis. Experimentation with new modes of preaching through digital media arts is taking place. Seminarians are aware of the multiple demands that will be placed on them in ministry and are being taught to commit themselves to spending the quality time needed to prepare their homilies. And finally, seminarians are learning to collaborate with laywomen and laymen in ministry. Hopefully, as priests they will seek ways to share the ministry of preaching with their lay colleagues.

There is no famine of the Word (Amos 8:11) and no shortage of need for preachers from all walks of life to break it open. The preparation of preachers is not only the responsibility of seminary faculty and staff; all the faithful have a role in encouraging the development of this essential ministry for the church. The reflection questions that follow explore the roles we all have in achieving this goal.

Questions for Reflection

1. What action is required to insure that biblical studies and homiletics maintain a central place in the seminary curriculum?
2. How can students be helped to move from exegetical study to proclamation of the Word?
3. How can professors help seminarians become appreciatively adept at using contemporary critical methods of biblical interpretation in their lifelong study of the Scriptures?
4. How can seminarians be helped to grow in their love of and prayer with Scripture?
5. What concrete, specific actions will enable seminarians to learn the skills and attitudes needed to preach to increasingly diverse congregations?

6. What are various ways seminarians might be led to construct homilies that are proclamations of Good News?
7. How can formal structures for input and feedback improve the quality of preaching?
8. How might seminaries and parishes prepare for the possibility of lay preaching?
9. What must happen to enable priests to have quality time for preaching preparation?
10. How can preachers make use of all the means of communication now available to proclaim the Word?

The Culture of Encounter
The Future of Seminary Formation

Msgr. Peter Vaccari

Rector, St. Joseph's Seminary and College, Dunwoodie
Yonkers, New York

The history of the church since the mid-1980s to the present confirms what the lives of the saints and sinners of every era teach. The church is a place where the drama of the sacred encounter between God and creation continues to unfold. In his first encyclical, Pope Benedict XVI wrote,

> We have come to believe in God's love: in these words the Christian can express the fundamental decision of his life. Being Christian is not the result of an ethical choice or a lofty idea, but the encounter with an event, a person, which gives life a new horizon and a decisive direction.[1]

All recent popes—Blessed Paul VI (1963–78), St. John Paul II (1978–2005), Benedict XVI (2005–13) and Francis (2013–present)—demonstrate a growing awareness and insistence on the integral importance of an authentic encounter with Jesus, the Word Incarnate, as the condition for one's fruitful identification as his disciple and member of his church.

This commentary, in three parts, asserts that a culture of encounter has emerged as a seminal development in programs of priestly formation.[2]

---

[1] Benedict XVI, *Deus Caritas Est* (2005) 1. Available at http://www.vatican.va/holy_father/benedict_xvi/encyclicals/documents/hf_ben-xvi_enc_20051225_deus-caritas-est_en.html.

[2] In 2012, St. Joseph's Seminary, the seminary of the Archdiocese of New York since 1896, became the single degree granting Catholic seminary for all of downstate New

The first part provides an overview of the movement toward a culture of encounter in seminary formation. The second part examines the impact of Pope Francis's understanding of the meaning of an authentic culture of encounter, especially in seminary formation programs. The final part looks toward the future of seminary formation.

The Emergence of a Culture of Encounter in Seminary Formation: Pope St. John Paul II's *PDV* (1992) and *PPF* (2005)

The 1992 apostolic exhortation of John Paul II, *PDV*, marked a seminal moment in the work of priestly formation. It identified the need and required candidates for the priesthood to integrate four pillars of formation: human, spiritual, intellectual, and pastoral.

PDV viewed the "deepest identity" of the seminary as rooted in "the apostolic community gathered about Jesus" (60). From a human perspective, it saw the seminary as a place offering the opportunity for deep friendship and joy. As an ecclesial community, the seminary should be "a community that re-lives the experience of the group of Twelve who were united to Jesus" (*PDV* 60). This foundational understanding of the life of the seminary means that proper attention must be given to an unambiguous affirmation of the role of formators to discern on behalf of the church what is for its good while at the same time attending to the needs of the "journeyer" in his particular circumstances (*PDV* 61).

Without using the language of encounter, *PDV* casts the process of formation in philosophical language and theological anthropology characteristic of the Thomistic personalism of its author, John Paul II. It articulated the trinitarian, christological, and ecclesiological foundations of the ministerial priesthood, ultimately pointing to its radical communitarian form (*PDV* 17). The priesthood is relational, oriented toward the bishop and united with members of the presbyterate. There is no theological basis for a "Lone Ranger" mentality. The priest is called to a

---

York. The three local ordinaries, Timothy Cardinal Dolan (archbishop of New York), Nicholas DiMarzio (bishop of Brooklyn), and William Murphy (bishop of Rockville Centre) formed an inter-diocesan partnership for seminary formation, ongoing priestly formation, and the offering of MA degrees in Theology for qualified laity and those in consecrated life. This included designating how each of the three arch/diocesan seminary properties was to be utilized in service of this cooperative vision. In effect, the arch/diocesan ordinaries modeled a unique form of a culture of encounter through their own analysis of the best practices for formation, faculty, and finances.

life of service. To realize this goal, he must be a man of communion, and with those whom he serves he must be a man of "mission and dialogue" (*PDV* 18). The language of *PDV* laid the theological foundations for the fifth edition of the *PPF.*

The first four editions of the *PPF* emphasized spiritual formation and included topics related to human formation. Some of the factors contributing to the fifth edition of the *PPF* included the publication of *PDV*, the mandated apostolic visitations of all United States seminaries ordered by John Paul II and voluntary seminary visitations, the sexual abuse crisis, the struggle of the church to build a "civilization of life and love" against the "culture of death," and many changing factors for the church in the United States at the beginning of the twenty-first century.

The 2005 *PPF* identified the pillar of human formation as the first pillar. Within the context of the human development of the candidate, it emphasized how the priestly personality is to be that of a "bridge and not an obstacle" (*PPF* V 75). It speaks of human formation as a process that involves growth in "self-knowledge, self-acceptance, and self-gift—and all this in faith" (*PPF* V 80).[3] This process seeks integration with the other dimensions or pillars of formation.

Pope Benedict XVI

The language of encounter is present in the first encyclical of Benedict XVI, *Deus Caritas Est*, as it makes clear that the deepest core of one's Christian identity is the choice made in light of an encounter with the person of Jesus Christ. In fact, Msgr. Peter Vaghi proposes the theme of "encounter with Jesus Christ" as the fundamental hermeneutic of Benedict XVI.[4]

In October 2010, Benedict XVI wrote an open letter to seminarians on the importance of seminary life. His point of departure is the identity of the seminary as the "community of disciples . . . who desire to serve the greater Church."[5] He invites seminarians to focus on three fundamental

---

[3] Here *PPF* V cites the USCCB Committee on Priestly Formation's *Spiritual Formation in the Catholic Seminary* (1982).

[4] Peter J. Vaghi, "Benedict XVI: The Theologian Pope," *OSV Weekly* 1 (May 22, 2012), https://www.osv.com/OSVNewsweekly/Article/TabId/535/ArtMID/13567/ArticleID/1363/Benedict-XVI-The-Theologian-Pope.aspx.

[5] Benedict XVI, Letter of His Holiness Benedict XVI to Seminarians, 2010, http://w2.vatican.va/content/benedict-xvi/en/letters/2010/documents/hf_ben-xvi_let_20101018_seminaristi.html.

areas. The first was "to live in constant intimacy with God"[6] through Eucharist, penance, and prayer in order to cultivate a deep interiority. Second, the pope urged seminarians to appreciate and apply themselves to study, not being distracted by whether certain subjects had immediate pastoral application. Finally, the pope noted that the seminary years should be marked by a period of growth toward human maturity. The pope places high priority on this value especially in relation to growth in human affectivity and its integration of the gift of sexuality. He underscores the dramatic urgency of this value in light of the way in which "some priests disfigured their ministry by sexually abusing children and young people."[7]

Pope Francis and the Culture of Encounter

In his Message for the 48th World Communications Day on June 1, 2014, Pope Francis spoke of the important role of the world of communications, especially social media and digital technology, in the promotion of a culture of encounter: "It is not enough to be passersby on the digital highways, simply 'connected'; connections need to grow into true encounters."[8] The promotion of a culture of encounter emerged as a major theme in the early pontificate of Pope Francis. It received perhaps its most elaborate development in his 2013 apostolic exhortation, *Evangelii Gaudium (EG)*.

Evangelii Gaudium and the Four Pillars of Formation

Professor Francesco Botturi, vice-rector of the Catholic University of the Sacred Heart of Milan, argues that the theme of a culture of encounter is central to *EG*. It develops, he suggests, in three stages. First, a phenomenology of encounter compels one to go out to become the missionary disciple. Second, an anthropology of encounter challenges one to risk going out of oneself to the other since we need others to fully realize ourselves. This encounter points to the paradoxical character of

---

[6] Ibid., 1.

[7] Ibid.

[8] Pope Francis, Message for the 48th World Communications Day, http://w2.vatican.va/content/francesco/en/messages/communications/documents/papa-francesco_20140124_messaggio-comunicazioni-sociali.html.

our existence reflected in the mystery of the incarnation.[9] The third stage is a pastoral and cultural economy of "encounter."[10] The language of Pope Francis here is important: having encountered the risen Jesus, we are to become "encounter."

EG uses the word "encounter" almost three dozen times, opening with the statement that "the joy of the gospel fills the hearts and lives of all who encounter Jesus" (1). The pope explicitly repeats the words of his predecessor, Benedict XVI, in affirming the acceptance of the Gospel as being rooted in encounter or renewed encounter with the love of God in Jesus Christ.[11]

EG was published for the universal church—for bishops, clergy, consecrated persons, and the lay faithful. However, it offers a worthwhile hermeneutic on the pope's thinking for those who discern a call to the priesthood. In what follows, highlights from the document have been selected and applied to the pillars of priestly formation. Two key hermeneutical principles are important: the pillars cannot be compartmentalized but must be integrated in the lives of the seminarians. Second, Pope Francis is a Jesuit whose theological vision is inseparable from his Ignatian spirituality. As James Martin, SJ, writes,

> For Ignatius, God is not confined within the walls of a church. Besides the Mass, the other sacraments and Scripture, God can be found in every moment of the day: in other people, in work, in family life, in nature and in music. This provides Pope Francis with a world-embracing spirituality in which God is met everywhere and in everyone.[12]

The worldview of Pope Francis is only intelligible through an appreciation of the discernment process of St. Ignatius that requires and expects one to enter into the discernment of God's will with a contemplative and imaginative, thoroughly detached heart. Yet, it can be a messy process,

---

[9] Francesco Botturi, "New Evangelization and Culture of Encounter," http://www.novaevangelizatio.va/content/nvev/en/international-meeting-summaries-of-presentations/nuova-evangelizzazione-e-cultura-dell-incontro.html.

[10] Ibid.

[11] Ibid., 7–8.

[12] James Martin, "How might Jesuit spirituality influence Pope Francis' papacy?," *America* (April 29, 2013), http://americamagazine.org/issue/article/his-way-proceeding.

filled with contradictory signs, fears, and many questions. *EG* appears to be the fruit of such a faithful and faith-filled, joyful process.

Applied to the meaning of seminary life and priestly formation, *EG* uses the experience of encounter with Jesus as the basis for one's joyful proclamation of the Gospel. It also forms a critical context for understanding many of Pope Francis's other comments directed toward seminarians.

PDV identified human formation as "the basis of all priestly formation" (43). Throughout *EG*, Pope Francis refers to the importance of the human component of our encounter with Jesus who walks with us. Acceptance of ongoing conversion, constantly listening to Jesus who desires to walk, breathe, and work with us must remain at the heart of missionary discipleship (*EG* 264–66). We must be convinced that we are in love with Jesus. The test of that union is that "we seek what he seeks and we love what he loves" (*EG* 267). In this way, we will never succumb to the temptation to be "that kind of Christian who keeps the Lord's wounds at arm's length. Yet Jesus wants us to touch human misery, to touch the suffering flesh of others" (*EG* 270).

In terms of the spiritual pillar of formation, the pope notes that the spiritual life must go much deeper than exercises that "offer a certain comfort but which do not encourage encounter with others, engagement with the world or a passion for evangelization." To remain spiritually within one's own comfort zone can result in "a heightened individualism, a crisis of identity and a cooling of fervor. These are three evils which fuel one another" (*EG* 78). The necessary antidote for the missionary disciple is a more contemplative life, a deep interior space. Such is filled by "prolonged moments of adoration, of prayerful encounter with the word, of sincere conversation with the Lord" (*EG* 262). The most powerful place of prayerful encounter is to be led by the Holy Spirit to the foot of the cross where we remain with Mary, the Mother of the church.

The culture of encounter also speaks to the intellectual pillar of formation. *EG* endorses a rigorous intellectual engagement as a necessary condition for the joyful proclamation of the new evangelization. Pope Francis insists the Gospel must be proclaimed

> to professional, scientific and academic circles. This means an encounter between faith, reason and the sciences with a view to developing new approaches and arguments . . . a creative apologetics which would encourage greater openness to the Gospel on the part of all. (*EG* 132)

The pope charges theologians to understand the vital link between theology and evangelization. It can never become a "desk-bound theology" (*EG* 133). He sees the homily and the various methods of study associated with it as indispensable for piercing and "joining loving hearts, the hearts of the Lord and his people" (*EG* 143).

Finally, the proclamation of the joy of the Gospel requires an enormous pastoral awareness, analysis, and nothing less than the zeal of missionary disciples. This deepens the importance of the pastoral pillar in seminary formation. The pope reminds priests, for instance, that the confessional "must not be a torture chamber but rather an encounter with the Lord's mercy" (*EG* 44). Integral to *EG* as well is the social justice dimension of the Gospel, especially the commitment of the missionary disciple to be in solidarity with the poor. Building on the work of his predecessors, John Paul II and Benedict XVI, Pope Francis is explicit in his language, "I want a Church which is poor and for the poor" (*EG* 198). The church's social doctrine is to permeate every aspect of life, for its principles seek to achieve "a peaceful and multifaceted culture of encounter" (*EG* 220).

Pope Francis on Seminary Formation

Pope Francis used two different occasions to emphasize to seminarians and their formators the importance of the culture of encounter. On July 6, 2013, the pope urged seminarians and novices to be aware of the seduction of the "culture of the temporary." In contrast, the pope recommended the true joy that "is born from the encounter, from the relationship with others . . . Joy is born from the gratuitousness of an encounter." Pope Francis counsels the seminarians and novices to be attentive to the spiritual, intellectual, apostolic and community pillars of seminary life and places particular emphasis on community life.[13]

Meeting with rectors and students of the Pontifical Colleges and residences of Rome in May 2014, Pope Francis returned to the theme of encounter in priestly formation. He emphasized the importance of being images of the Good Shepherd. To do this requires the human capacity to enter into the experience of encounter. In fact, he stresses the importance

---

[13] Pope Francis, Meeting with Seminarians and Novices, July 6, 2013, http://w2 .vatican.va/content/francesco/en/speeches/2013/july/documents/papa-francesco _20130706_incontro-seminaristi.html.

of "the mysticism of encounter,"[14] which involves the ability to hear and to listen to others.

What the Future Might Hold

This commentary has argued that priestly formation, from the mid-1980s to the present, has seen a development around the value of a culture of encounter. A significant turn in this direction occurred with the introduction of the integrative importance of the four pillars of formation in *PDV* in 1992. Since then, programs of priestly formation have highlighted the importance of the role of human formation, the language of encounter, and the desire for a genuine culture of encounter. Many factors have contributed to this development: sociocultural, philosophical, theological, the need for even greater vigilance and transparency in light of the sexual abuse crisis, and the pursuit of the best means to promote the new evangelization. In light of these developments, I would offer four observations about what the future might hold.

First, a fundamental, if not *the* fundamental, theme of the Second Vatican Council was the universal call to holiness for a church engaged in the sanctification of the world. The last thirty years have been marked by the leadership of three popes whose memories extended back to Vatican II. Two of those popes participated in the council itself as theologians. They each developed unique philosophical-theological-pastoral perspectives within the same ecclesial orbit. This is a critical point for seminary formation, that is, the reality of changing patterns of formation within the mystery of the same church. Seminarians and formators alike must always have before them the axiom *sentire cum ecclesia* (to think with the church) and not be distracted by personal agenda.

Second, the fastest-changing reality for the church and its seminaries comes from the questions posed by the digital world to faith, theology, and the transmission of ideas in our culture. In 2012, Fr. Antonio Spadaro, Jesuit theologian and editor of the prestigious journal *La Civiltà Cattolica*, was interviewed by the director of the Vatican newspaper, *L'Osservatore Romano*. When asked about his interest in the impact of the digital world, he replied,

[14] Pope Francis, Address to Rectors and Students of the Pontifical Colleges and Residences of Rome, May 2014, http://w2.vatican.va/content/francesco/en/speeches/2014/may/documents/papa-francesco_20140512_pontifici-collegi-convitti.html.

The Web and the cyberspace culture are calling into question our ability to formulate and to listen to a symbolic language that speaks of the possibility and signs of transcendence in our life. Perhaps the time has also come to consider the possibility of what I call a "cybertheology," in other words, the knowledge of faith in the Web era. It is the fruit of faith that releases a cognitive impulse in an epoch when the logic of the Web is marking the way of thinking, knowing, communicating and living.[15]

The digital world is not just the latest modality of communication. It is the world in which we live, where ideas are exchanged, emotions developed and expressed, and where priestly formation occurs. Its impact on priestly formation cannot be overestimated and learning how to navigate that world alert to its possibilities and challenges is an essential part of the work of seminaries.

Third, the future is now. The culture of encounter is the next seminal shift in the area of priestly formation. Will a revised *Ratio Fundamentalis* and a revised sixth edition of the *PPF* reflect this seminal development toward a culture of encounter? Seminaries continually examine themselves in terms of their mission to form priests filled with holy zeal who are about the lifelong process of the integration of the four pillars or dimensions of formation. The intelligibility of that process rests with an openness to enter into the logic of the culture of encounter. The dynamic of that encounter, in our global and digital world, is the locus where the church fulfills her mission to proclaim the Gospel of merciful love and tenderness.

Finally, we need to draw on the example and intercession of Mary and the saints. They demonstrate for us how the church in every age has given a glimpse of cultures of encounter between the mystery of God and our human pilgrimage. In *EG*, Pope Francis compares intercession to "leaven" in the heart of the Trinity. "It is a way of penetrating the Father's heart and discovering new dimensions that can shed light on concrete situations and change them" (283).

In an alcove just outside the main chapel in the hallway of St. Joseph's Seminary in Yonkers, New York, there is a replica of Michelangelo's *Pietà*.

---

[15] Antonio Spadaro, SJ, interviewed by director of *L'Osservatore Romano*, *Vidimus Dominum*, January 26, 2012, http://www.vidimusdominum.org/en/index.php?option=com_content&view=article&id=605:todays_digital_revolution_affect_faith&catid=5:reflection&Itemid=19.

It has served for generations as a reminder to all who have seen it of the encounter between sin and God's tender mercy. In the work of the new evangelization and the joyful proclamation of the Gospel, Pope Francis, following his predecessors, recommends Mary's maternal intercession. This is not just an expression of piety. The pope reminds us,

> She [Mary] constantly contemplates the mystery of God in our world, in human history and in our daily lives. She is the woman of prayer and work in Nazareth, and she is also Our Lady of Help, who sets out from her town "with haste" (Lk 1:39) to be of service to others . . . We implore her maternal intercession that the Church may become a home for many peoples, a mother for all peoples, and that the way may be opened to the birth of a new world. It is the Risen Christ who tells us, with a power that fills us with confidence and unshakeable hope: "Behold, I make all things new" (Rev 21:5).[16]

[16] *EG* 288.

Appendices

Appendix 6-B: Sacred Scripture Credits

Appendix 6-C: Systematic/Dogmatic Theology Credits

Appendix 6-D: Moral Theology Credits

Appendix 6-E: Historical Studies Credits

Appendix 6-F: Pastoral Theology Credits

Appendix 1-A:

Theological Schools:
Enrollment of Seminarians, 1961–62 to 2014–15

Year	Total Seminarians	Diocesan Seminarians	Religious Seminarians	Number of Seminaries	Average Enrollment
1961–62	8,480	--	--	134	63
1971–72	6,089	3,864	2,225	67	91
1981–82	3,813	2,649	1,164	53	72
1991–92	3,432	2,536	896	49	70
2001–2	3,584	2,621	963	45	80
2011–12	3,723	2,805	918	41	87
2013–14	3,631	2,784	847	39	93
2014–15	3,650	2,799	851	39	94

Substantial changes occurred in both the numbers of seminarians and of seminaries/schools of theology between 1961–62 and 1971–72. The number of seminarians dropped by nearly 2,400, from 8,480 to 6,089 (-2,391) and the number of seminaries by exactly half, from 134 to 67 (-67). Meanwhile, the average enrollment increased from 63 to 91 in the ten-year span (+28), even though the institutions were still very small. The next decade, from 1971–72 to 1981–82, a comparable decrease of 2,276 students occurred and the average number of seminarians per school declined to 72 per school. The number is somewhat higher (94) in 2014–15. In addition, some 2,861 lay students are currently enrolled, boosting the average to 166 students per school. It was during the 1970s that lay students were first admitted to theological schools, a trend that grew through the years. They are, however, distributed unevenly, leaning toward enrollment in religious order schools rather than diocesan seminaries (CARA data, 1961–2015).

Appendix 1-B:

Vatican II Documents with Occasional Mention in the Five Editions of the *Program of Priestly Formation*

Edition Document	1st	2nd	3rd	4th	5th
Dei Verbum (Dogmatic Constitution on Divine Revelation)	4	3	4	2	2
Sacrosanctum Concilium (Constitution on the Sacred Liturgy)	3	3	2	1	1
Gaudium et Spes (Pastoral Constitution on the Church in the Modern World)	2	3	--	--	1
Dignitatis Humanae (Declaration on Religious Liberty)	1	1	--	--	--
Ad Gentes Divinitus (Decree on the Church's Missionary Activity)	2	3	1	--	1
Apostolicam Actuositatem (Decree on the Apostolate of Lay People)	--	--	1	1	--
Perfectae Caritatis (Decree on the Up-to-Date Renewal of Religious Life)	2	3	--	1	1
Christus Dominus (Decree on the Pastoral Office of Bishops in the Church)	4	8	4	1	2
Unitatis Redintegratio (Decree on Ecumenism)	6	5	4	1	1

Appendix 1-C:

Use of Other Documents in the Five Editions of the *Program of Priestly Formation*

Edition Document	1st	2nd	3rd	4th	5th
Pastores Dabo Vobis (1992) I Will Give You Shepherds	--	--	--	85	76
Codex Juris Canonici (1983) Code of Canon Law	--	--	--	23	91
Ratio Fundamentalis Institutionis Sacerdotalis (1970) Basic Scheme for Priestly Training	3	10	4	8	6
Sacerdotalis Caelibatus (1967) On the Celibacy of the Priest	--	--	--	3	--
Ecclesiae Sanctae (1966)	1	8	1	--	--
On the Governing of the Holy Church	--	--	--	--	--

Appendix 1-D:

Bishops Who Served on *PPF* Committees: Age in 1962

PPF Edition	Average Age	Range of Ages	Median Age
1st	49	33 to 65	49
2nd	41	28 to 53	42
3rd	37	28 to 53	34
4th	28	22 to 34	28
5th	16	5 to 23	15

Appendix 1-E:

Pope Who Named the Bishops Who Later Served on *PPF* Committees

PPF Edition	Pius XI	Pius XII	John XXIII	Paul VI	John Paul II
1st	1	7	6	9	--
2nd	--	--	1	12	--
3rd	--	--	--	10	--
4th	--	--	--	2	6
5th	--	--	--	--	11

Appendix 1-F:

References to Vatican II by General Categories, Seminary Catalogs 1982–85 to 2012–14 (35 Seminaries)

Category	Early 1980s	Early 2010s
History and Purpose of the School	16	8
Formation	12	11
Other	11	20
Total	39	39
References by Discipline	166	213
GRAND TOTAL	205	252

Appendix 1-G:

References to Vatican II by Discipline, Seminary Catalogs 1982–85 to 2012–14 (35 Seminaries)

Discipline	Early 1980s	Early 2010s
Church History	32	29
Sacraments and Worship	33	34
Theology (Systematic)	53	105
Theology (Moral)	8	20
Ministry/Pastoral	30	15
Sacred Scripture	5	3
Spirituality	5	7
TOTAL	166	213

Appendix 2-A:

Theologate Ownership and Operation

Owned and Operated by an Archdiocese or Diocese (15)

St. John's Seminary, Camarillo, CA: Archdiocese of Los Angeles

St. John Vianney Theological Seminary, Denver, CO: Archdiocese of Denver

University of St. Mary of the Lake/Mundelein Seminary, Mundelein, IL: Archdiocese of Chicago

Notre Dame Seminary, New Orleans, LA: Archdiocese of New Orleans

Saint John's Seminary, Brighton, MA: Archdiocese of Boston

Sacred Heart Major Seminary, Detroit, MI: Archdiocese of Detroit

Saint Paul Seminary School of Divinity, St. Paul, MN: Archdiocese of St. Paul/Minneapolis

Kenrick-Glennon Seminary, St. Louis, MO: Archdiocese of St. Louis

Immaculate Conception Seminary School of Theology, Seton Hall University, South Orange, NJ: Archdiocese of Newark

Christ the King Seminary, East Aurora, NY: Diocese of Buffalo

Saint Joseph's Seminary, Yonkers, NY: Archdiocese of New York

Athenaeum of Ohio/Mount St. Mary's Seminary of the West, Cincinnati, OH: Archdiocese of Cincinnati

Saint Mary Seminary and Graduate School of Theology, Wickliffe, OH: Diocese of Cleveland

Saint Charles Borromeo Seminary, Wynnewood, PA: Archdiocese of Philadelphia

University of St. Thomas School of Theology at St. Mary's Seminary, Houston, TX: Archdiocese of Galveston-Houston

Owned and Operated by Religious Orders for Dioceses (7)

Holy Apostles College and Seminary, Cromwell, CT: Missionaries of Holy Apostles in collaboration with Connecticut bishops

Saint Meinrad Seminary & School of Theology, St. Meinrad, IN: Benedictine monks of Saint Meinrad Archabbey

St. Mary's Seminary & University, Baltimore, MD: Sulpicians

Mount Angel Seminary, St. Benedict, OR: Benedictine monks of Mount Angel Abbey

Saint Vincent Seminary, Latrobe, PA: Benedictine monks

Oblate School of Theology, San Antonio, TX: Oblates of Mary Immaculate

Sacred Heart Seminary and School of Theology, Hales Corners, WI: Priests of the Sacred Heart

Owned and Operated by Religious Orders for Religious Orders (9)

Dominican School of Philosophy & Theology, Berkeley, CA: Western Dominican Province

Jesuit School of Theology of Santa Clara University, Berkeley, CA: US Jesuit Provinces

Franciscan School of Theology at University of San Diego, CA: Franciscan Friars, St. Barbara Province

Dominican House of Studies, Washington, DC: Dominican friars and brothers

Catholic Theological Union, Chicago, IL (multiple): Owned by a corporation, sponsored and operated by twenty-four men's religious communities, as well as other communities who send students to CTU

Moreau Seminary at University of Notre Dame, Notre Dame, IN: Indiana Province of the Holy Cross

Boston College School of Theology and Ministry, Chestnut Hill, MA: US Jesuit Provinces

Saint John's School of Theology and Seminary, Collegeville, MN: Benedictines of Saint John's Abbey

Aquinas Institute of Theology, St. Louis, MO: Dominicans of the Province St. Albert the Great

Other Arrangements (8)

St. Patrick's Seminary & University, Menlo Park, CA: Owned by the Archdiocese of San Francisco and operated by the Sulpicians

The Catholic University of America, Washington, DC: Owned and operated by USCCB

St. Vincent de Paul Regional Seminary, Boynton Beach, FL: Owned by the seven dioceses and bishops of the Province of Florida and operated by diocesan priests

Pope St. John XXIII National Seminary, Weston, MA: Owned by a corporation and operated by diocesan and religious priests

Mount St. Mary's Seminary, Emmitsburg, MD: Owned by a corporation and operated by diocesan priests

Ss. Cyril & Methodius Seminary, Orchard Lake, MI: Owned by a corporation and conducted by diocesan priests

Pontifical College Josephinum, Columbus, OH: A Pontifical institution subject to the Holy See, owned by a corporation and operated by diocesan priests

Pontifical North American College, national seminary in Rome: Owned and operated by USCCB

Appendix 3-A:

Highest Academic Degree of Those Serving as Academic Deans

	1989	*1999*	*2015*
PhD	20	15	17
STD/SSD	13/1	11	12/1
JCD/EdD	1	1	1
DMin	0	2	2
Other Doctorates	2	2	4
Percent Doctorates	**77.1**	**92.5**	**94.9**

SSL	0	6	1
STL	4	2	2
JCL	2	0	0
Master's	5	1	0
Percent without Doctorates	*22.9*	*7.5*	*5.1*
*In both 1989 and 2015, one person held both a PhD and an STD			
**Other doctorates include: ThDr, DrT, DThM, HED, TD, JD, and DPhil			

Appendix 3-B:

Academic Rank of Those Serving as Academic Deans

	1989	*1999*	*2015*
Professor	11	9	16
Associate Professor	12	15	11
Assistant Professor	7	9	6
Instructor	0	0	1
Rank not given	19	7	5

Appendix 3-C:

Vocational Status of Those Serving as Academic Deans

	1989		*1999*		*2015*	
	Number	*Percent*	*Number*	*Percent*	*Number*	*Percent*
Diocesan priests	23	49.0	15	37.5	12	30.8
Men religious*	21	42.9	18	45.0	12	30.8
Laymen	3	6.1	4	10.0	12	30.8
Women religious	1	2.0	3	7.5	2	5.1
Laywomen	0	0	0	0	1	2.6
*All are priests except one who is a brother.						

Appendix 3-D:

Academic Field of Those Serving as Academic Deans

	1989	1999	2015
Systematic Theology	12	10	10
Theology (field not specified)	5	3	1
Scripture	8	7	5
Pastoral Theology	4	6	5
Spiritual Theology	0	0	3
Moral Theology	3	4	7
Church History	5	3	5
Other*	3	3	3
Church/Canon Law	3	2	0
Not specified	0	4	0

* 1989—Religious Education, Psychology, Education; 1999—Psychology 2, Education; 2015—Philosophy 3.

Appendix 6-A:

Credit Distribution by Year for the Master of Divinity Degree

				Courses	Required
	1987	1997	2015	Required*	by PPF
Sacred Scripture	17.6	17.1	17.8	6	6
Systematic (Dogmatic) Theology**	26.6	30.5	34.2	11	15
Moral Theology	11.2	10.5	11.8	4	4
Historical Studies (Church History)	8.6	8.9	9.8	4	3
Pastoral Studies	23.9	22.5	24.1	8	12
Field Education (Supervised Ministry)	11.8	10.8	10.0	variable	2
General Electives/Other	8.0	11.9	9.8	3 or 4	some
Total credits required	107.7	112.2	117.5		

* Courses required refers to the average number of courses currently required in the particular field; required by the *PPF* refers to the number of areas of study required in the *PPF* V.

** Includes credits in Sacraments, Liturgy, and Spirituality.

Appendix 6-B:

Sacred Scripture Credits

Number of credits per school: 2015	Average credits overall	1987	1997	2015
10–12 hours = 3 schools				
13–15 hours = 9 schools	Mean	17.6	17.1	17.8
16–18 hours = 14 schools	Median	18	18	18
19–25 hours = 11 schools	Mode	19–21	18	18
>25 hours = 1 school	Range	12–28	12–26	10–27

Appendix 6-C:

Systematic/Dogmatic Theology Credits*

Number of credits per school: 2015	Average credits overall	1987	1997	2015
15–18 hours = 16 schools	Mean	11.2	10.5	18.6
19–22 hours = 22 schools	Median	11	10–11	19
	Mode	12	12	21
	Range	6–24	6–18	15–22

* In addition to the 18.6 credits in Systematic/Dogmatic Theology, in 2015 Spirituality credits equaled 3.1 and Sacramental/Liturgical Theology equaled 12.5 credits for a total of 34.2 credits.

Appendix 6-D:

Moral Theology Credits

Number of credits per school: 2015	Average credits overall	1987	1997	2015
5–6 hours = 3 schools				
7–9 hours = 5 schools	Mean	11.2	10.5	11.8
10–12 hours = 20 schools	Median	11	10–11	12
13–15 hours = 6 schools	Mode	12	12	12
>15 hours = 4 schools	Range	6–24	6–18	5–21

Appendix 6-E:

Historical Studies Credits

Number of credits per school: 2015		Average credits overall	1987	1997	2015
5–6 hours	= 5 schools	Mean	8.6	8.9	9.8
7–9 hours	= 13 schools	Median	7–9	9	10
10–12 hours	= 19 schools	Mode	6	6	9
>12 hours	= 1 school	Range	3–15	3–14	5–15

Appendix 6-F:

Pastoral Theology Credits

Number of credits per school: 2015		Average credits overall	1987	1997	2015
12–13 hours	= 2 schools				
14–18 hours	= 5 schools	Mean	23.9	22.4	24.1
19–24 hours	= 10 schools	Median	24	22.5	25
25–30 hours	= 16 schools	Mode	24	23	25
>30 hours	= 5 schools	Range	9–38	12–37	12–34

Bibliography

Alberigo, Giuseppe, and Joseph A. Komonchak, eds. *History of Vatican II, Vol. 4: Church as Communion: Third Period and Intersession, September 1964–September 1965.* Maryknoll, NY: Orbis Press, 2003.

Confoy, Maryanne. *Religious Life and Priesthood: Perfectae Caritatis, Optatam Totius, Presbyterorum Ordinis.* Mahwah, NJ: Paulist Press, 2008.

Congregation for Catholic Education. *Guidelines for the Study and Teaching of the Church's Social Doctrine in the Formation of Priests.* 1988.

Faggioli, Massimo. *Vatican II: The Battle for Meaning.* New York: Paulist Press, 2012.

Flannery, Austin, ed. *Vatican Council II: Constitutions, Decrees, Declarations; The Basic Sixteen Documents.* Collegeville, MN: Liturgical Press, 2014.

Francis, Pope. *Evangelii Gaudium.* Vatican City: Libreria Editrice Vaticana, 2013.

Gaillardetz, Richard, and Catherine Clifford. *Keys to the Council: Unlocking the Teaching of Vatican II.* Collegeville, MN: Liturgical Press, 2012.

Gautier, Mary L., and Thomas P. Gaunt. *Celibacy Formation and New Faculty Formation in the Program of Priestly Formation: A Report to the USCCB Secretariat of Clergy, Consecrated Life and Vocations.* Washington, DC: CARA, Georgetown University, February 2015.

Gautier, Mary L., Thomas P. Gaunt, and Jonathon L. Wiggins. *Liturgical and Spiritual Formation in Seminary Programs: A Report to the USCCB Secretariat of Clergy, Consecrated Life and Vocations.* Washington, DC: CARA, Georgetown University, March 2014.

Gautier, Mary L., and Mark M. Gray. *Formation in Catechesis and Evangelization and Ecumenical and Interreligious Relations in Seminary Programs: A Report to the USCCB Secretariat of Clergy, Consecrated Life and Vocations.* Washington, DC: CARA, Georgetown University, March 2013.

Gautier, Mary L., and C. Joseph O'Hara. *Justice and Equality: Formation in Catholic Social Teaching and Intercultural Competency in Seminary Programs: A Report to the USCCB Secretariat of Clergy, Consecrated Life and Vocations.* Washington, DC: CARA, Georgetown University, May 2012.

Hoge, Dean. *Experiences of Priests Ordained Five to Nine Years: A Study of Recently Ordained Catholic Priests.* Arlington, VA: NCEA, 2006.

———. *The First Five Years of the Priesthood: A Study of Newly Ordained Catholic Priests.* Collegeville, MN: Liturgical Press, 2002.

Hoge, Dean, and Jacqueline Wenger. *Evolving Visions of the Priesthood: Changes from Vatican II to the Turn of the New Century.* Collegeville, MN: Liturgical Press, 2003.

John Paul II, Pope. *Pastores Dabo Vobis.* Vatican City: Libreria Editrice Vaticana, 1992.

Keller, James, and Richard Armstrong, eds. *Apostolic Renewal in the Seminary in the Light of Vatican II: The Program of Priestly Formation.* New York: Christophers, 1965.

Lee, James Michael, and Louis J. Putz, eds. *Seminary Education in a Time of Change.* Notre Dame, IN: Fides, 1965.

McCarthy, Jeremiah, Mark Latcovich, et al. (in collaboration with the ATS). *An Assessment Workbook.* Pittsburgh: ATS, publication forthcoming.

O'Malley, John W. *What Happened at Vatican II.* Cambridge, MA: Harvard University Press, 2008.

———. *Trent: What Happened at the Council.* Cambridge, MA: Harvard University Press, 2013.

Papesh, Michael. *Clerical Culture: Contradiction and Transformation.* Collegeville, MN: Liturgical Press, 2004.

Poole, Stafford. *Seminary in Crisis.* New York: Herder and Herder, 1965.

Sanks, T. Howland. "Education for Ministry since Vatican II." *Theological Studies* 45 (September 1984): 481–500.

Schuth, Katarina. "Fully Understanding the Moment and Embracing the Future: Seminary and Religious Candidates." In *To Be One in Christ: Intercultural Formation and Ministry,* edited by Fernando Ortiz and Gerard McGlone. Collegeville, MN: Liturgical Press, 2015.

United States Conference of Catholic Bishops. *Co-Workers in the Vineyard of the Lord: A Resource for Guiding the Development of Lay Ecclesial Ministry.* Washington, DC: USCCB, 2005.

———. *Preaching the Mystery of Faith: The Sunday Homily.* Washington, DC: USCCB, 2012.

———. *Program of Priestly Formation.* Washington, DC: USCCB, 1971, 1976, 1981, 1992, 2005.

Wheeler, Barbara G., and Helen Ouellette. *Governance That Works: Effective Leadership for Theological Schools.* Auburn Studies series. New York: Auburn Theological Seminary, March 2015.

White, Joseph. *The Diocesan Seminary in the United States: A History from the 1780s to the Present.* Notre Dame, IN: University of Notre Dame Press, 1989.

Index

academic deans, 57–58, 180–82

academic programs, 100–112. *See also* intellectual formation

administration, 48–60; changes, 60; other administrators, 57–60. *See also* academic deans; rectors/presidents

admission, 16, 58–59, 77–78, 89, 93, 120

advisers. *See* formation, directors

advisory boards. *See* boards

apostolic visitation of seminaries, 32, 37, 40–41, 61, 89, 97, 103, 108, 125, 145, 166

assessment, evaluation, 46, 112, 120

Association of Theological Schools (ATS), 4–6, 118

Benedict XVI, Pope, 164, 166–67, 170

Bible. *See* Sacred Scripture

bishops, role in development of PPFs, 14–15, 18–19, 23–24, 27–29, 68, 78, 111, 144, 177

boards, 42–48; committees, 45; development, 120; functions and responsibilities, 44–48; structure and membership, 43–44

canon law, 22–23, 111–12

catechesis, 110, 133–34. *See also* religious education

celibacy, sexuality, 92–94, 95, 98, 106, 126, 152; spiritual training, 16–17

Center for Applied Research in the Apostolate (CARA), xvi, 4, 75–76, 80–81, 108, 175. *See also* justice

church, alienated Catholics in the United States, 118, 144–45; call to holiness, 171; generational differences, 132–38; ministry, 162–63; signs of the times, 127–28, 144–45; universality, 126–27. *See also* parish

church history. *See* historical studies

clericalism, anticlericalism, 127–28

Clinical Pastoral Education (CPE), 31–32, 113

Code of Canon Law. See canon law

collaboration, 85–87, 94, 119, 156–57, 161–62

college, pre-theology, 119, 124–25

Co-workers in the Vineyard of the Lord, 87, 102, 119

critical methods. *See* historical studies; Sacred Scripture

culture. *See* multicultural, intercultural

Cupich, Archbishop Blase J., xi–xiii

curriculum. *See* formation programs

187